Mike,

If you can dream it, and you can live it. The future is what we make it!

All the best.

[signature] 12/2012

FEARLESS RETIREMENT

CONRAD TONER, B.A., CFP CLU

FEARLESS RETIREMENT

HOW TO RETIRE WITHOUT FINANCIAL WORRY!

CONRAD TONER, B.A., CFP CLU

Fearless Retirement
© 2012 Conrad Toner

All rights reserved. No part of this book may be reproduced or transmitted in any form or by any means, electronic or mechanical, including photocopying, recording, or by any other information storage and retrieval system, without written permission from the author, except for the inclusion of brief quotation in a review.

The scanning, uploading and distribution of this book via the Internet or via any other means without the permission of the author is illegal and punishable by law.

Note to reader:
The information in this publication does not constitute a recommendation for the purchase or sale of any securities. The author and publisher are not engaged in rendering investment advisory, legal, accounting or financial planning services through this publication. If such assistance is required, readers should seek the individual advice of a professional.

Publisher:
Financial Doctor Press, Inc.
Peterborough, ON
Canada

First Edition
ISBN: 978-0-9869093-0-6

Cover design by: Joni McPherson of McPhersonGraphics.com
Book design by: Sue Balcer of JustYourType.biz
Edited by: Bruce McDougall of BrucerMedia.com

Printed in 2012

www.FearlessRetirement.com

Dedication

This book is dedicated to my father, the late Gerald F. Toner. He was a great man truly dedicated to the craft of writing. He demonstrated this throughout his entire career as a newspaper man. Yet he never got to fulfill his own dream of writing a book, something he was going to do when he retired. That chance never came as he was taken from us at the age of 57.

Although I didn't know it at the time, dad influenced me in a wonderful way through his tragic death. He was a consummate planner. And because of that, our family was able to survive "financially" when he died so young. It was his example of careful forethought that allowed the fear and anxiety I felt at 18 to eventually guide me into the field of financial planning.

Dad we've missed you terribly for a very long time. At times this book has been a real struggle to complete. It was during those times I would remember the words you used to say whenever times got tough……..

"Illegitimi non carborundum"

Thanks dad…this one's for you.

Contents

Preface xi

Part 1: Challenges 1

Introduction 3

Chapter 1: A new perspective 9
The latest boomer research, trends and numbers. What's it all gonna cost?

Chapter 2: Traditional retirement risks 17
Boomers will face a number of risks in retirement. The more common ones are: market, inflation and interest-rate risk. But a few other risks are even more important.

Chapter 3: Risks of the NEW retirement 29
Longevity, health care and sequence of return will have an impact on your retirement. Here's how.

Chapter 4: Death of a salesman 39
The traditional stockbroker or financial advisor has typically done a good job of helping boomers amass a pile of assets to use in retirement. Now you need to focus on capital preservation for the purpose of providing guaranteed income for the next 30 years.

Chapter 5: An industry at fault 49
There are several reasons why industry regulations don't protect you.

Part 2: Solutions   59

Chapter 6: Investment projections are not retirement income plans   61

You need a retirement income plan, but what the heck is that? One thing it isn't: an investment projection.

Chapter 7: The four planning cornerstones   67

Money for the short, medium and long term and a backup plan, form the four cornerstones of a sound retirement plan.

Chapter 8: The psychology of retirement income planning   79

How to use psychology to determine what you will be spending in retirement, and where that money should come from.

Chapter 9: The new math of retirement   105

Out with the old, in with the new: Why simple asset allocation isn't enough when positioning your assets to generate income in retirement.

Chapter 10: Financial advisor checklist   123

Check, check, check: Here's a detailed checklist to protect your money and a simple way to help find the right advisor for you.

Chapter 11: Fees, fees and more fees — what are they all for?   169

Don't know what you're paying or if it's too much? A better question to ask is: What value am I getting for the fees I'm paying?

Chapter 12: Planning or transaction focused? The Planning Scorecard   193

Transaction-based or planning-based: How does the advisor shape up?

Chapter 13: Mixing math with psychology, the working chapter: 205

Bringing Maslow's hierarchy together with product allocation makes for a perfect marriage when creating your retirement income plan.

Chapter 14: Bringing it all together   251

A final word on achieving your retirement dream.

Appendix 1: 255
Long Term Care Insurance and Retirement Income Insurance defined

Appendix 2: 263
A designation comparison from FINRA

Appendix 3: 269
Worksheets

Statement of Disclaimer 275

Preface

As you can tell from the title, this is a book about retirement. But you shouldn't write it off as just another one of those books that's going to tell you how much you must save for the retirement of your dreams. **Fearless Retirement** really is different. Here's what it's not about.

First of all, this is not a book about investments. You won't find the latest get rich quick investment scheme in this book. Nor will you find information about how to invest in the stock market, how to buy and sell real estate, how to set up your own home-based business or how to become a savvy day trader. It's not about the latest wonder product that's going to help you retire fabulously wealthy. And it isn't written for people who want to learn how to start saving for their future retirement. It's for people who are almost ready to retire and have already done the saving.

If investment advice or saving strategies aren't the focus of the book, then what is? The short answer is that this book focuses on the transition between your working years to the next stage of life. For lack of a better term, we commonly use the word retirement to describe this next stage. But retirement today is nothing like the retirement of yesteryear. It's no longer as cut and dried as it once was, when you worked to a certain age then stopped working and then lived a few golden years playing golf and visiting the grandkids. This retirement thing has changed significantly in the past few years, and it will continue to be reshaped in many unknown and exciting ways as baby boomers enter this next phase of life.

Fearless Retirement will prepare you for this major life transition. The book focuses primarily on the financial aspects of your preparation. But it will also help you to discover what you want to do when you no longer go to work every day and how you'll pay for it all. You may work part-time or you may not. That chapter of your life has yet to be written. The point is when you retire (whatever that means to you), your life will change and you need to plan for that change. When you no longer get a paycheck, you'll still have bills to pay, probably for many more years than you've ever considered. In fact, one of the biggest fears that people have about their retirement is the fear that they'll run out of money. How will you ensure that your money lasts as long as you do?

In this book, I'll show you how to take stock (pardon the pun) of where you are today. I'll also help you to create a solid plan so that your money will last for the rest of your life. I'll help you identify what you are going to do, how much it will cost, and where you'll get the money.

One of the keys to a fearless retirement involves protecting your money so it can provide you with a lifelong income. To do this, you first need to know what factors put your money at risk. Then you have to learn how to eliminate or at least reduce those risks. In this book, I'll show you how to do both these things.

Specifically, I'll provide you with insights into the 7 key risks that you need to avoid if you want to make a successful transition. Then I'll provide a framework that you can use to create a lifelong income from the money you've already saved for retirement. If you like to handle your own investments, I'll provide the tools you'll need to create your own plan. If you'd rather have a root canal than handle the details of your financial plan, I'll teach you how to find the right financial advisor to do the planning for you.

The steps in this book are simple and practical. To make them easy to follow, I've included some worksheets and a few links to web-based resources. Once you create your own Fearless Retirement Income Plan, you can focus in the next stage of your life on things that really matter, without worrying about outliving your money.

The planning concepts and solutions discussed in the book are universal. They apply no matter where you live. I refer to Canadian products and use Canadian terminology, but that's because I live and work in Canada - Eh! If you're not Canadian, you can still use this book to create your own retirement income plan. When the time comes to put your plan into action, you'll simply select appropriate products available in your country.

Part 1
Challenges

Introduction

Today is one of those rare lazy Saturdays when there is nothing pressing to do. Work's been crazy lately, so a day without any responsibility has come as a godsend, and I've have been taking full advantage of it. Sitting on my porch I've been reading the newspaper, coffee in hand, while a gentle rain falls. Occasionally I glance up from the paper to watch the world go by, and that's when I see it. A brilliant, colourful and vibrant rainbow has formed across the sky. It seems to begin right in front of my house, and yet the other end is so far off in the distance, I can't quite get a handle on where it ends. One thing's for sure: it is the closest I have ever been to a rainbow, and the colours are absolutely magnificent.

Just then a gentle breeze blows with that sweet smell of spring. You know the one I'm talking about. "Ahh." I love the smell of spring. And then it hits me like a ton of bricks. The breeze, the brilliant colours and that smell have instantly transported me back in time to childhood, one of those vivid memories of days past, magically triggered by three distinct senses colliding in time. I feel as if I am really there. I'm six years old again, full of innocence, with not a care in the world.

I'm running across a field with my best friend, the tall

grass lapping at my legs and the wind in my face. The two of us are desperately trying to get to the end of that rainbow. But no matter what we do, we never seem to make it. It's almost as if we're running on a treadmill. It completely eludes us. And just as when I was six, I can't seem to understand why. From a distance it looks like there are two ends, but they just don't seem to touch the earth anywhere.

Now another memory pops up clear as a bell. I am suddenly overwhelmed with a strange feeling of urgency. I've heard the stories about a pot of gold at the end of the rainbow. What six-year-old wouldn't want one of those? I think to myself, "I must keep going if I am ever going to find that pot of gold."

As quickly as it came, the rainbow disappears, and the pot of gold vanishes into thin air. For a couple of moments I feel sad and disappointed, just as I did all those years ago. But then, like the rainbow, my trip down memory lane disappears as well.

"Wow," I think, "that was weird. Funny how a simple smell can trigger such detailed memories."

Now I'm back to the present reality, and I'm not really six anymore. But then I have a revelation! I may not be six anymore, but I am still on that darn treadmill, chasing the pot of gold at the end of the rainbow. I've been working for more than 30 years toward that elusive goal called retirement. And just like the pot of gold at the end to the rainbow, I have no idea where it is or how I am going to get to it. Worse, I have no idea how much is in the pot or how long it might last if I ever grab hold of it.

My eyes drift back to the business section of the newspaper. The first thing I see as I turn the page is an ad for a retirement planning seminar. It's promoting some new wonder product from XYZ Financial something or other. The ad is kind of catchy, so I go ahead and read it. I think to myself, they're just going to try to sell me more stuff. I don't need any more stuff! What I need is help with the financial stuff I already have, so I can figure out where I go from here. I don't want to work forever, but I don't really know how or when I can afford to pull the plug on work. And when I do, I have no idea if my money will last for the rest of my life. There has to be a better way to deal with this thing called retirement, but just like the pot of gold, the better way seems hidden away somewhere.

> If you're a boomer on the cusp of this transition called retirement, you need to stop chasing the next great product peddled by your bank, broker or advisor and get back to the basics.

There is a way to find that pot of gold

I don't think anyone would disagree that life has become far more complicated than it used to be. The concept of retirement and the whole industry behind its promotion is no exception. For years we have been taught that life is about working until a certain age, and then we'll be free to golf, garden or travel as if we're on a permanent vacation. That vision of retirement has been promoted by the financial services industry, which has designed all its products to help us achieve it.

The financial services industry has prompted us to save, save and save some more, because someday we'll need to replace our income when we stop working. But even the so-called experts can't agree on how much of our income we'll need to replace in retirement.

There's a fundamental flaw with this traditional model of retirement that nobody seems to talk about. Not only has life become much more complex, but we face many new realities and risks as we enter this next phase of life. On top of this, the industry and its participants are not doing enough of what must be done to help us make this transition. In fact, with every passing year, they seem to come up with more products, each one more complicated than the last. The financial services industry, try as it might, has not been able to shift its focus away from products and selling. But products alone are not the solution to help people make this major life transition successfully.

If you're a boomer on the cusp of this transition called retirement, you need to stop chasing the next great product peddled by your bank, broker or advisor and get back to the basics. Before you even consider pulling the plug on work, you have to answer two fundamental questions:

First, what are you going to be doing in this next phase of your life?

Second, how much is it all going to cost and how will you pay for it?

The answer to living the second half of life without worrying about running out of money doesn't lie in the latest wonder product. It comes far before you look at any product at all.

You start with something much more basic than the complex solutions offered by the financial industry and its salespeople. It's based on time-tested and effective concepts and principles. Rather than loading up on the product of the day first and then wondering if it's the thing that will help you achieve what you want in life, the secret is to start with a plan.

This plan will help you determine first the kind of life you want and then how much that life might cost and where the money will come from to pay for it. Then and only then can you identify the products you'll need to get where you want to go. Unfortunately, most people put the financial cart before the horse, and that is largely the fault of the financial services industry.

Chapter 1: A New Perspective

You've been working for 30+ years and now you're starting to count the days until you can retire. Or maybe you've just crossed over into this next phase of life. If you're like many people, you've focused mostly on when this day would come. But have you ever given much thought to what you'll be doing from now on and how long you might be doing it? I don't mean just the big things, like travel and the retirement projects you may have planned. I'm talking more about the repetitive, common, everyday things that you'll be doing. On a more philosophical note, what will your new life purpose be, once you no longer have to report to work?

To help you with this, let's look at the following set of numbers. The numbers illustrate a very important aspect of your life after work. Once you understand what they represent, they will give you a new perspective on this second phase of your life, which you've been working towards for years. Go ahead, read the numbers and take your best guess as to what they might represent. Just write your answer in the space provided.

1,561 _____

32,871 _____

360 _____

10,957 _____

262,968 _____

So how did you make out? Did you figure out most of the answers? If you missed a few, that's OK. You can check out the complete list of answers at the end of this chapter, or visit **www.FearlessRetirementResources.com**. You'll also find some additional examples on the website.

The purpose of this book is to help you create a plan for the next 10,957 days of your life. Why 10,957 days? One of the new challenges that you face today in retirement is a much longer life expectancy. Studies show that a person who reaches 60 to 65 today could live for another 30 years. If that's the case, then 10,957 represents the number of days in a 30-year period, including leap years.

All the other numbers on the last page represent either periods of time, the number of times you might do something, or certain costs associated with living over a 30-year period. Why am I sharing this seemingly useless trivia? To help you change your perspective about your retirement. Many people focus just on getting to the date when they can retire, so they can quit work permanently. Some focus on the big trip or project they have planned. Yet most don't give much thought about what they might do after they retire, from day to day. Nor do they consider how long they might be doing it, what it all might cost and how they'll pay for it.

By looking in this way at the next stage of your life, you can begin to think about it in a whole new light. This is especially true for the financial end of retirement. When you start adding up all the basic things you'll need to pay for, let alone the large purchases of cars and trips, you'll realize that you should do some figuring before you get there. Some of the numbers may seem pretty big, and I don't mean to scare you with them. Keep in mind that this exercise will project certain costs over 30 years. You won't have to come up with the money all at once.

> **When you start adding up all the basic things you'll need to pay for, let alone the large purchases of cars and trips, you'll realize that you should do some figuring before you get there.**

The concept of retirement used to be about working to age 55, 60 or 65 and then saying, "That's it, that's all, we're done work now." This notion was based on the experience of our parents or grandparents and on what the financial services industry has been telling us for years. The industry has told us to envision a new life of leisure. After all, we've paid our dues, right? Some people envision golfing every day or lots of travel. Others see the golden years simply as a time to relax, with no major responsibilities, tasks or deadlines.

This made sense when you could expect to live only to 72 if you're retired at age 65. I've even heard that, when the Canada Pension Plan (CPP) was first introduced in Canada, the government didn't expect many workers to live long enough to collect it at age 65.

Things are different now. As I mentioned, if you retire at 65, you can expect to live for as long as another 30 years. When factored with other trends of the new retirement, this 30-year period will be quite different than our parents' and grandparents' retirement. Not only are boomers expected to live much longer, but the things they are likely to do in retirement will be quite different as well. To paraphrase an old marketing slogan from Buick, "This ain't your father's retirement."

Most people would agree that the baby boomer generation has reshaped many industries during its journey since the late 1940s. And there's no reason to believe this trend won't continue right into retirement and beyond. As boomers age, their spending power and the number of votes they control will allow them to demand changes in many areas of their lives. So what will this new retirement look like? How will boomers shape it? No one knows for sure, but some of the areas bound to be affected include:

- Where boomers live and how many places they call home.

- How boomers work: Many will likely continue to work, but it will be on their own terms, because they choose to, not because they have to. This may be a part-time job, contract work or even a new home-based business.

- How boomers spend their time: Some will want to do volunteer work for which they never had the time while working.

- What they do for vacations: They will likely place much more emphasis on adventure vacations, especially in the earlier years of retirement.

- Who they need to care for: Many boomers will need help caring for an elderly parent (either in their own home or in a facility).

- At the same time as caring for their parents, many will be helping to look after their grandchildren.

- How they envision the future: When they get to the stage of needing help themselves, they have no desire to live in a traditional retirement or nursing home. They envision a much more holistic and community-based approach. In living out their final years, they will emphasize care with dignity.

Answers to the Numbers Quiz

10,957   The number of days in 30 years including 7 leap years
 1,561   The number of weeks in 30 years

32,871	The number of meals prepared in 30 years (3 per day)
360	The number of months in 30 years to pay monthly utility bills
60	The number of bi-annual visits to the dentist
262,968	The number of hours in 10,957 days

Real Life Example

Let's consider the experience of one of my clients from my financial consulting business. (The names and occupations in my examples have been changed to protect their privacy.) Angela worked her whole life in the dental health field and retired at age of 60. Throughout her working years, Angela had always been a saver, and she managed to retire with a sizeable investment portfolio that would help supplement her government and work pensions. She never spent beyond her means and lived a very modest lifestyle. But now that she was finally free of work, she had big plans to do some traveling, albeit within her budget.

For the first couple of years, Angela went to many of the places she had dreamed of visiting. She seemed to be living her dream. Every time I spoke with her she was planning another trip. Then one day I got a strange call from her. She asked me where she should put her RRSP contribution for the year. I was puzzled. I told her that there was no need for such a contribution now that she was retired. Angela said she had returned to work. I was shocked. I said that she could always start drawing on her retirement funds if she was worried about funding her trips.

Her reply gave me my first glimpse into the reality of the boomers in this new age of retirement. "You don't understand!" she said. "I'm bored when I'm not out traveling, and there's only so much gardening and housework to do. So I've accepted a part-time position with a new dentist. When he interviewed me, I told him all the things that I didn't want to be responsible for, the tasks I was no longer willing to do, and that there would be times when I'd need a month off to travel. I couldn't believe it when he said yes. So now I get to do the part of the job I used to love, none of the job I hated to do, and come and go as I please. On top of it all, I feel that I still have a purpose in life, and I can help people without any of the heavy burden and responsibility that I used to have."

Chapter 2: Retirement risks

Clearly this new retirement is going to look different than retirement in the past. Whether or not you give up your paycheque completely or only partially in the early part of this next phase of life, you'll face certain financial risks. And unlike your parents and grandparents, you'll have to deal with some new ones. There's even a new phrase to describe this period in the boomers' lives: The Retirement Risk Zone.

The five or so years leading up to retirement and the first five years of retirement constitute the key zone. During this period, boomers will need to pay much more attention to these risks and come up with solutions to avoid or mitigate them. By doing so, they can construct the worry-free retirement they've long dreamed about.

Dispensing with big technical definitions let me define risk in very simple terms as it pertains to your retirement:

A risk is anything that may keep you from living the retirement lifestyle that you've envisioned.

You've worked hard and saved to get to this stage in life, and now you just want to enjoy it. But a number of things could affect your financial security or force you to change your lifestyle, whether you want to or not. Together, they add up to one main concern: a fear that you will run out of money before you run out of life.

Anyone entering retirement today or in the foreseeable future faces seven major risks. Three of them would be considered traditional risks that many generations have dealt with. These are:
Market Risk
Inflation Risk, and
Interest Rate Risk

Four other risks affect the current generation, particularly the boomers. These other risks are:
Longevity Risk,
The Cost of Future Health Care
Sequence of Return Risk, and
Financial Advisor Risk

In this chapter, I will discuss the first three traditional risks.

Market Risk

Whenever I conduct live seminars, I always discuss the risks people will face in retirement. Generally I begin by asking the attendees what they think the major risk is to their financial well being during retirement. Almost without fail, the majority say it has something to do with the markets. The perception seems to be that if their retirement nest egg is invested in the markets, their life savings could be wiped out with the next big market crash or correction.

While it's true that being invested in the stock market (either directly or through mutual funds or segregated funds) does ex-

> A risk is anything that may keep you from living the retirement lifestyle that you've envisioned.

pose your money to risk, this is one risk that is quite manageable. I'll discuss this more in a later chapter.

Fluctuations in the markets are not the problem. The real risk comes from the reaction of individual investors to these inevitable ups and downs in the market. By no means am I going to give you a Ph.D course in financial markets. If you're inclined to learn about the technical aspects of market risk, there is no shortage of material available to teach you about beta coefficients, Sharp ratios and the like. All that stuff aside, what you really need to understand about the markets is actually quite simple. If you understand these few simple concepts, you'll be well on your way to letting the markets assist you and protect your wealth. But you must start by getting past all the noise and hype that the industry and media propagate about the markets.

In simple terms, the following phrases summarize the basic concepts that you must know about the markets before you can profit from them.

1. Markets go up and markets go down.

2. They go up more than they go down.

3. The ups and downs are repeatable cycles.

4. Buying low and selling high is better than the reverse.

5. Time in the market is more important than "timing the market".

Logically, these simple statements make perfect sense. Why, then, have many people who have invested in the markets had such a negative experience?

The short answer is human behaviour. As humans, we let emotion rather than logic drive our decisions. The emotions of fear and greed drive our decisions of when to get in and when to get out of the market. Understanding that emotions drive our decisions and having a non-emotional investing system in place will improve our experience in the markets.

FIGURE #1

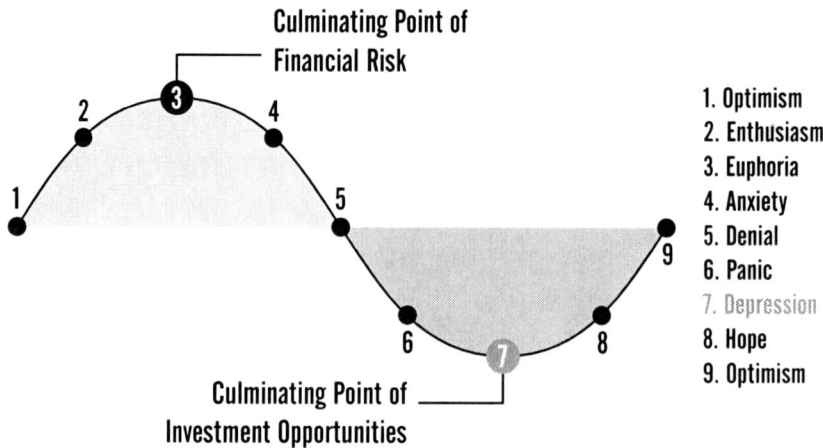

Source: Industrial Alliance Investment Management Inc., used with permission

Figure #1 could represent the cycle of just about any investment, including gold, silver, real-estate. It could even represent the life cycle of a particular stock market, exchange traded fund, or mutual fund. For this example, let's assume it represents a mutual fund marketed by a financial advisor. What is important to note is not so much the up-and-down nature of the graph, but the emotional reactions at the various stages.

This example shows how emotion often overrides the logic of investing. Remember the five simple concepts from above: buy low, sell high, time in the market, etc? Does any of this seem familiar? Have you ever experienced this?

Don't feel bad if you have experienced something like this, because you are not alone. A company named Dalbar & Associates actually tracks this behaviour. In one of their studies, called "Quantitative Analysis of Investor Behavior", they looked at investors' behaviour and their investment return over a 20-year period compared to the performance of certain mutual fund categories and investment indices. The results are quite compelling and show that individual behaviour, driven by psychological factors, has far more influence than the markets themselves on poor performance.

One of their studies for a specific 20-year period found that the average investor's experience was far worse than that of the mutual-fund categories in which they might actually have invested. (See Table 1 below) This indicates that the underlying mutual funds, invested in stocks available in markets around the world, were not the problem. If the average investor made only 4.3% compared with 9% in the average Canadian equity fund over the same period, then the investor simply didn't stay invested. It is not the markets but the movement in and out of funds at the wrong time that causes this kind of poor result.

Table 1: Investment returns of selected mutual funds and an individual investor

	Average CDN Equity Fund	Average US Equity Fund	Average Global Equity Fund	Average CDN Bond Fund	Average Investor Experience
20 years	9%	7.4%	7.2%	7.3%	4.3%

Source: Globe HySales, based on Globe Peer Indices as of Dec. 31, 2006; Average Investor – Dalbar

So just why do people behave this way? Quite simply, they want to buy when they feel good about buying or when they feel safe. And they want to sell when they don't feel good or safe anymore. Unfortunately, this is often contrary to the principle of buy low, sell high. When markets are low, people don't feel safe. When markets are high, they do. So they end up buying at the top, when they feel good (safe), and selling at the bottom, when they've had enough and feel bad.

Mutual fund companies only make matters worse. Mutual fund and other financial companies do not advertise their products after they've just experienced a –15% year. They advertise when they enjoy a +15% year. They want to look good, so they promote themselves when they have positive numbers to present. As the chart in figure #1 demonstrates, when you buy at the top, your investments have only one way to go.

Many financial advisors get caught up in this as well. For some, the only value proposition they bring to their clients is to recommend investments on an ongoing basis. So when they meet with their clients for the annual investment review they may very well recommend some changes. But what do you think they are likely to recommend? Will it be the fund that just went down 15% or the one that went up 15%? More often than not, it's the fund with the positive number, because on some level the advisors' own emotions play a part in this situation, as well. Advisors figure a client will not buy into a loser – the fund that just went down 15% – even though they know logically this would be the best option. Advisors conduct much of this activity simply to show the client that they're doing something to earn their fees. Let us not forget the Dalbar study.

A major downturn in the markets is certainly a risk and could have a very negative impact on your investment portfolio. But the market's activity is really out of our control. Our reactions to the market's activity and our behaviour are ultimately within our control. If we can alter our behaviour and follow a non-emotional investing system, then we can profit from the market in the long run.

Inflation

We all know about inflation, and we know that it affects the cost of the goods we buy and consume. On a year-to-year basis, we see the price of groceries, gas, clothing, and just about everything else going up. But most of us don't consider the effect of inflation over longer periods. When I discuss this topic in my live seminars, I always ask the audience a very pointed question to illustrate this point.

Keep in mind that my audience usually consists of people aged 55 to 75. Here's the question:

"How many of you here today paid more money for your last car than you paid for your first house?"

After a bit of laugher, some uneasiness and some discussion among the attendees, a significant number (40%-50%) without fail will answer yes to this question. In a nutshell their experience demonstrates the major impact of inflation over time. As you proceed into the next 10,957 days, you cannot expect anything different.

We can also look at the cost of a basket of groceries over time. Let's say a typical weekly trip to the local shopping centre costs you $200. This includes groceries, toiletries, pet food and other supplies. How much would you expect this same basket of groceries to cost in, say, 10, 15, 20 or even 30 years? The answer will depend, of course, on the inflation rate in the future. As a point of reference, the Figure 2 shows the history of inflation in Canada from 1915-2005.

Chapter 2: Retirement Risks 25

Figure 2: Inflation History 1915 -2005

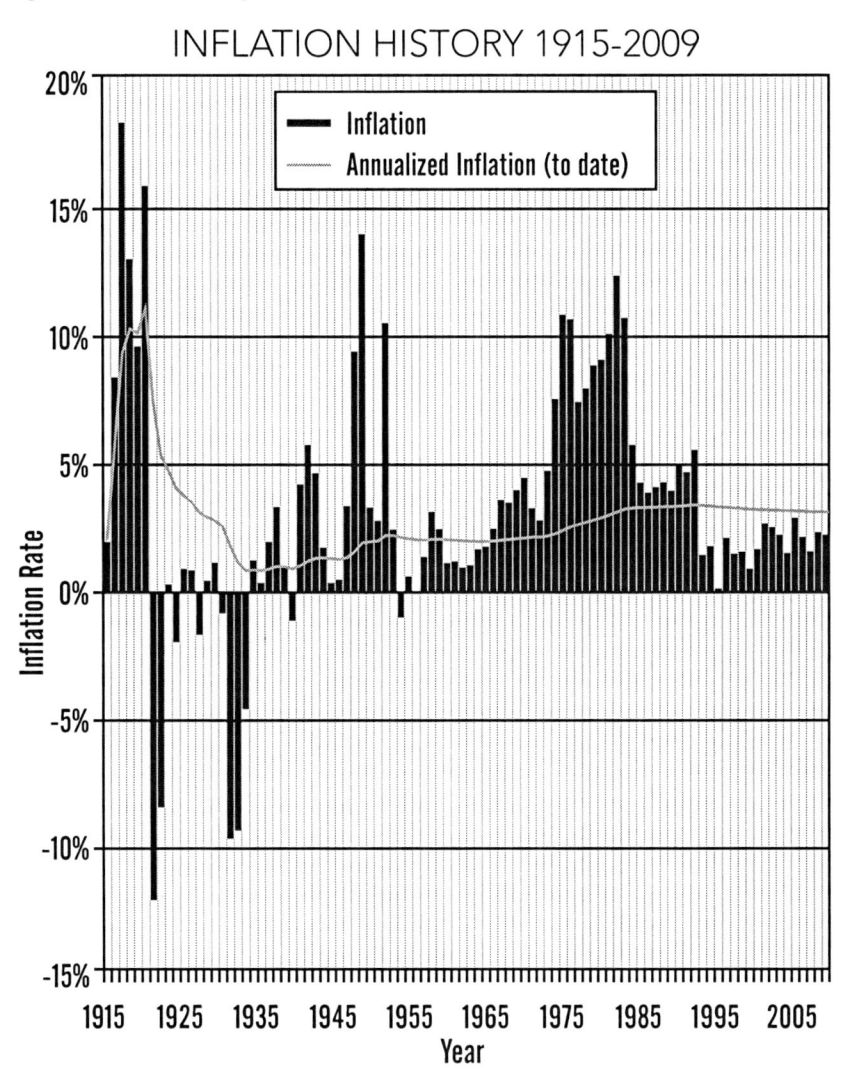

INFLATION HISTORY 1915-2009

— Inflation
⋯ Annualized Inflation (to date)

Inflation Rate

Year

Inflation History data obtained from Statistics Canada.

Clearly it's not possible to predict exactly how much things will cost at any specific point in the future. As Figure 2 shows, these numbers vary from year to year. The best we can do is to assume a simple average rate of inflation to give us an approximation. Doing so, Table 3 shows how much a basket of goods that you buy today for $200 will cost in 10, 15, 20 and 30 years, if we assume inflation of 3% and 5%.

Table 2: Effect of inflation on the cost of a basket of goods

Today's Cost	Inflation Rate	10 Years	15 Years	20 Years	30 Years
$200	3%	$268.80	$311.60	$361.20	$485.40
$200	5%	$325.80	$415.80	$530.60	$864.40

The bottom line with respect to inflation is that things will continue to cost more in the future than they do today. If inflation averages 3%, the $200 you spend at the market today will almost double 20 years from now. Depending on how long you live, inflation will have a significant impact on your financial resources and could even annihilate them, depending on your specific situation.

Interest Rate Risk

In general, as people get older they tend to become more conservative. With respect to investing, this is certainly true. As people age, they also perceive their future in shorter periods. While their perceptions are true to a degree, the average investor tends to invest for these shorter periods a bit too early, often starting around the time of retirement. In fact, the financial services industry encourages us to switch our investments into fixed-income instruments as we get closer to retirement. Some rules of thumb attempt to gauge how much fixed income we should have, based on our age. One such rule states that the percentage of fixed income in our portfolio should equal our age.

Part of a well-rounded investment strategy, admittedly, should include some fixed-income investments. A problem arises, however, for people who put too much into short-term fixed income investments. GICs or CDs earn their return as interest rather than dividends or capital gains. Although the capital is largely protected, these investments are subject to interest rate risk. Interest rate risk works like this:

> If inflation averages 3%, the $200 you spend at the market today will almost double 20 years from now.

Say I invest in a five-year GIC at a current rate of 3.5%. My money is now locked up for five years. Sure, it's guaranteed, and I have a predictable 3.5% return. But what happens if in two years the interest rate on GICs increases to 6%? I have to sit on the sidelines and wait another three years before I can get that 6%, right? Well sort of. If rates are still at 6% in three years, I can reinvest at 6%. But if they come down again, I'm out of luck. In other words, if you lock in when rates are low, you risk losing out on higher returns.

On the other hand, let's say you get a five-year GIC at 6%, when rates are high. That's a good thing for the next five years. But when you reinvest after five years, the rates may be lower. One year rates may have fallen to 1.4% and five-year rates to 3%. If you reinvest now, you have to either take a short term and hope that rates go up or take the longer term and earn half as much as you'd done over the previous five years.

You can offset this risk by using a laddered GIC or CD strategy, investing in each of a series of GICs or CD's with maturity dates ranging from one to five years. In this way, a portion of your GIC/CD portfolio always matures each year. If rates are up, you can take advantage of them. If they're down, only a portion of your portfolio is invested at the lower rate.

Chapter 3: Risks of the NEW retirement

Aside from the traditional risks described in the previous chapter, four other risks could have a greater impact on your ability to live the retirement of your dreams. These four new risks are:
Longevity Risk
The Cost of Future Health Care
Sequence of Return Risk, and
Financial Advisor Risk

I will cover three of them in this chapter. Financial Advisor Risk requires a chapter of its own, and it comes after this one.

Longevity Risk

In the early 1900s, life expectancy of Canadians was around 47 years. Throughout the last century life expectancy has continued to climb. By the end of WWII it had risen to 63 years for men and 66 years for women. Today a couple who reach age 65 have a 94% chance of one partner living to age 80, and a 65% chance of one partner living to age 90.

Past generations never had to plan for, or fund such a long retirement. This new reality will require an income that may be needed for 30 years. As a result retirement savings will need to last that long in order to create the income. When you add longevity into the mix with some of the other risks, this last phase of life could pose significant financial challenges.

As we discussed earlier, inflation will inevitably affect purchasing power, particularly over long periods of time. If you expect to live 30 years in retirement, you need to account for the rising cost of living that will accompany such a long life.

Cost of Future Health Care

Certainly it is good news that we can expect to live longer than past generations. If we could all expect to live healthy and vibrant lives right to the end, this would be wonderful, too. When I suggest to clients or attendees of my seminars that they may live into their 90s, I often get a response like, "Gee, I hope not. I don't want to sit around drooling on myself in some old folks home."

No doubt we're living longer because of healthier lifestyles and great advances in medical technology, but eventually many of us will need some type of health care. The cost of this health care could pose a serious risk to our financial security.

The World Health Organization (WHO) recently added a new twist to life expectancy numbers. The WHO created the **D**isability **A**djusted **L**ife **E**xpectancy (**DALE**). Essentially, the DALE takes into account the fact that many people will become ill in their final years and will require some form of care. According to a WHO report, a female in Canada with a conventional life expectancy of 82 would have a DALE of 74, meaning that at age 74 she will likely start experiencing some form of health issue that requires care. A male with a conventional life expectancy of 78 can expect to have a DALE of 70.

If you're like most people, your reaction to such statistics may be, "But it won't happen to me". I certainly hope it doesn't. But studies show that 48% to 68% of people over the age of 65 will require some form of long-term care in their later years. (The Society of Actuaries, in a study called "Modification of National Nursing Home Survey" (1997) puts the number at 48%. In 2003, AARP put the number at 68% in *"A Report to the Nation on Independent Living and Disability".* Take your pick.)

If these numbers prove correct, a large percentage of boomers will need significant resources to obtain some form of care during an eight-year period of their retirement. This raises two questions: How much will this care cost? And how will you pay for it?

That's like asking, How long is a piece of string? The answer will depend on a number of factors, including: the severity of the medical issue, whether the care is provided in your home or in a facility, who provides the care, how long it is required, and where you live. To give you a sense of what such care might cost, let's look at a couple of scenarios based on someone who lives in Ontario, Canada.

An Example of in-home care:

Let's assume that someone requires care and decides to stay in his home. During a typical week, he requires the services of either a registered nurse (RN) or a licensed practical nurse (LPN) to monitor his health status and administer medication. In addition he requires the services of a personal support worker for bathing and dressing every day. And because he is staying in his own home, he requires someone to clean, shop and maintain the property. Table 3 shows how much this might cost given certain wage rates as of 2010 and estimated hours of service. As you can see the cost of just 34 hours of care out of the 168 hours in a week is $57,792 per year. This is, of course, in addition to the other regular household and lifestyle expenses he would normally incur.

Table 3: Weekly cost of in-home care: Ontario Provincial Median

	Home Care Services	Hourly Cost	Time Required	Total Cost Weekly
	RN/ LPN	$54.76	10 Hours	$547.60
	Personal care	$23.95	14 Hours	$335.30
	Home Management	$22.85	10 Hours	$228.50
Total/Week			34 hours/wk	$1,111.40/week
Total/Year			1768 hours/yr	$57,792.80/year

Source of costs for home care services: Taking Care Inc. October 2010

An Example of Facility Care in Canada

What about folks who have to move out of their homes and into a long-term-care facility? Like home care, the cost of a facility will vary depending on where you live and the level of care required. For instance if you simply couldn't manage the maintenance on your home and wanted to have meals prepared for you, you may choose to move to a retirement residence. Many consider this to be akin to an apartment with meals provided.

Some retirement residences offer special services for people who are functionally dependent, who can't perform two or more of the activities of daily living without substantial assistance. Of course, this comes at an additional cost. In Ontario, for instance, these homes are privately owned, and the cost is not subsidized by the government. The residents are responsible for all costs. The approximate average cost in Ontario for functionally dependent residents is shown in Table 4.

Table 4: Monthly Cost for Retirement Homes In Ontario

Room Type	Provincial Median	Provincial Range	Toronto Median	Ottawa Median
Private	$2,930.00/month	$1,329.00 - $7,750.00	$4,186.00	$3,275.00
1 Bedroom Suite	$3,727.50/month	$2,400.00 - $9,000.00	$3,888.50	$3,850.00

Source: Taking Care Inc. October 2010

As residents require more care, they are eventually moved to a nursing home. In Ontario, these homes are owned by a variety of organizations. Unlike retirement homes, applications to a long-term care home are controlled by the local Community Care Access Center (CCAC). Funding comes from the provincial Ministry of Health and Long-Term Care. The portion of the cost that the resident pays is called a co-payment. Like the retirement residence, long-term care homes charge different rates for different types of accommodation.

Table 5 lists the costs in the province of Ontario for long-term care as of October 2010.

Table 5: Cost of long-term care in Ontario

Long-Stay Program	Type of Accommodation	Co-Payment Daily Amount	Co-Payment Monthly Amount
Basic/Standard Accommodation	Various styles (depending on when the home was constructed or renovated)	$53.23	$1,619.08
Preferred Accommodation	Semi-Private Room	$61.23	$1,862.41
Preferred Accommodation	Private Room	$71.23	$2,166.58
Short Stay Program		$34.63	$1,053.33

Source: Taking Care Inc. October 2010

The above costs are for basic accommodations only and include furnishings, meals, bed linens and laundry, personal hygiene supplies, medical/clinical supplies and devices, housekeeping, pastoral services, social and recreational programs, medication administration (but not the cost of medicines), assistance with the essential activities of daily living, as well as 24-hour nursing and personal care and access to a physician and other health care professionals. Additional services like clothing, hairdressing, cable TV, telephone and transportation are not included.

If your income doesn't cover accommodation, a subsidy is available from the ministry, but only for the basic/standard room. To qualify, the CCAC conducts an income test based on the resident's income tax returns. If you qualify, your total monthly income, less $100, will be taken to cover the cost of a basic bed, and the balance will be covered by the provincial government.

As you can see from these examples, long-term care can cost a significant amount of money, regardless of where you actually receive the care. If you have the assets and resources to pay for it, you have nothing to worry about. If you don't, then you may face a significant financial challenge. If you're like many people, this is something you probably haven't considered, much less prepared for. This is why the future cost of long-term health care may in fact be one of the biggest risks you face in retirement.

Sequence of Return Risk

Earlier I discussed market risk. I said that the market itself isn't really the problem, but people's reactions to market movements that cause them grief. That's certainly true when you're accumulating your wealth for retirement. If you let your emotions guide you, you'll end up pulling out at the wrong time. But there's another market-related risk that can be even more serious for those about to retire or who are already retired and want to start spending their money. The industry calls this sequence of return risk.

Sequence of return describes the order in which you earn negative versus positive returns. It becomes a problem only when you're taking money out as income, not when you're accumulating funds. Here's what I mean:

Each of the following number sequences represents investment returns over a three-year period. If you look closely, you'll notice that two of the sets of numbers are the same, but are presented in reverse order.

+27%, +7%, -13% ....
-13%, +7%, +27% ....
+7%, +7%, +7% ....

Over the three-year period, each sequence generates exactly the same average rate of return: 7%. So why does the sequence of return matter?

When you are saving money, it doesn't matter. In fact if you're purchasing investments along the way to retirement, a few negative returns early on work to your advantage, because you can purchase additional units or shares more cheaply.

Sequence of return becomes a problem when you start selling some of your investments to generate income during retirement. Let's say you are 65, you have $100,000, and you want to generate a $9,000 annual income. In any year that you get a negative return, you will be forced to sell off more of your investments to generate $9,000. In the positive years you'll have to sell off less. Furthermore, the more negative years you have early in the sequence, the less time your money will last.

Now we'll look at the way each sequence determines how long your money will last after you turn 65. Keep in mind that we are assuming the sequences simply repeat themselves.

- In the 7, 7, 7 scenario, your money will last for 21 years, until you are 86.

- In the 27, 7, -13 scenario, your money will last 9 years longer, until you turn 95.

- In the −13, 7, 27 scenario, your money will run out by the time you turn 81. By reversing the sequence in which your investments generate these returns, you lose 14 years of income.

The bottom line is that you want to have as many strong positive years as possible early on, so that your money will last longer. Unfortunately this is totally and completely out of our control. We might as well just roll the dice and hope that lady luck is on our side.

Notably, this risk begins at some time before retirement, possibly even five or ten years earlier. You never know where you will be in the sequence of returns as you approach retirement. A person who'd planned to retire in 2006, for example, would have enjoyed two or three pretty good years leading before retirement, but the next two years were awful. What affect will this have on her money and how long it will last? Or what about someone who retired in 2008? Really, this risk needs to be addressed some time before retirement.

Chapter 4: Death of a salesman

As if it isn't enough for boomers to deal with the risks we've already discussed, we have to deal with one more. Our financial advisor is the person we turn to for help in managing our money. Unfortunately, we face the risk of getting poor advice from our advisor. In the worst case, our advisor may even commit theft or fraud, leaving us as his penniless victims.

The following news headlines sum up the worst consequences that can arise from this particular risk:

"Financial advisor gets jail term"
"Two local financial advisors are given lifetime ban by Securities Commission"
"Authorities can't find the money"
"Local advisor declares bankruptcy"

I am in no way suggesting that these headlines apply to all financial advisors. When it comes to advice, there are degrees of good and bad. Many excellent people work in this field, but there are a few bad apples. As a financial advisor myself, headlines like these reflect on my profession and, unfortunately, seem to be more common these days.

Financial advisor risk may also arise with an advisor who's very qualified, gives good advice, but does not specialize in what you need – retirement income planning. No matter how good an advisor is at helping you accumulate your money for retirement, his advice may be worthless or damaging if he doesn't know how to address all the issues and the risks in the retirement risk zone.

So who am I talking about when I say "financial advisor"? For the purpose of this book, I'm not referring to an official title bestowed by a regulator, but rather to a generic term for someone who advises on financial matters. Financial advisors go by many names, which can be confusing. These names include: investment advisor, broker, financial consultant, mutual fund salesperson, insurance salesperson, and financial planner. To keep it simple I'll try to refer to them all generically as financial advisors.

> **No matter how good an advisor is at helping you accumulate your money for retirement, his advice may be worthless or damaging if he doesn't know how to address all the issues and the risks in the retirement risk zone.**

You face a fundamental challenge in the structure of the financial advisory business that can negatively affect your ability to fund the next 30 years of your life. This challenge arises from two fundamental problems.

First, the majority of advisors in the industry today have been trained to help clients accumulate money, not spend it. In the past, this hasn't necessarily been a bad thing, because you had to amass your retirement savings to retire – right?

Second, advisors have conventionally been paid with commissions for transactions and fees for managing money. They have not been paid for assisting clients with financial or retirement planning.

These two elements are a deadly combination for someone who's about to retire. They're especially worrisome if you want to retire with complete confidence that you can live the lifestyle you want without worrying about running out of money.

Accumulating vs. Spending

There are two distinctly different periods in the average person's investing lifetime. One occurs when they are working at accumulating a pot of money to use in the future. The other occurs when they are spending the money they've accumulated. These two periods require distinctly different investment and management strategies.

Unfortunately, many financial advisors simply don't distinguish one period from another. As a result they don't provide the proper solutions to generate a lifelong sustainable income for their retired clients. This becomes very apparent during a cyclical market meltdown. During the market correction of 2008, everyone seemed to be discussing how retirees' portfolios had been devastated. Some had lost 50% to 60% of their portfolio's value, and yet these folks still needed to draw an income from their assets. Some people delayed their retirement or went back to work just to meet their fixed expenses, let alone pay for the things they planned to do once retired. The Canadian federal government even introduced a new rule allowing people to reinvest as much as 25% of their RRIF holdings that they had to withdraw if they were over age 71, in an effort to gain back some of the losses they had incurred.

Articles in the media blamed financial advisors. In some cases, I agree with those comments, although financial advisors didn't cause the market downturn. However, advisors who used accumulation strategies to manage their clients' money and who did not provide full retirement income planning advice really should be held accountable.

From a typical client's perspective, retirement income planning shouldn't be all that complicated. Once someone is going to draw on her investment assets, it only makes sense that she has a different strategy in place so all of her money isn't at risk when the next correction comes, as it surely will. This begs the question: Why isn't this being done as a matter of course by all so-called financial advisors? The answer to this simple question is complex.

There are a number of reasons why many advisors aren't doing the job that their clients hired them to do. The top five are:

- They don't know how.

- They don't want to do financial planning, which a client at this stage of life really requires.

- They don't have the time, and they blame this on increasing paperwork from all the regulatory requirements.

- They won't make the effort – this stuff takes a lot of time and effort.

- They don't get paid as much.

They Don't Know How:

OK, many of today's advisors have spent their career helping people amass a pot of money to eventually use in retirement. Some have even grown up alongside their clients, and they themselves are close to retirement. This has required a certain set of skills and mindset, and over the years they've become very good at it. But helping clients switch to managing how they spend their money requires a whole new mindset, with a different set of skills and new products. It isn't rocket science, but it does require some learning on the part of the advisor.

Probably the biggest challenge for many of these advisors is their resistance to change. It's not so much that they can't learn about the new strategies and products required for their clients, but that they don't want to make the changes necessary to learn about them. And that's OK, too, as long as they're willing to step aside and make room for advisors who'll do what is needed to help their clients manage how they spend their money.

As the saying goes, you can't teach an old dog a new trick. This becomes most apparent with financial advisors who work as traditional stockbrokers. Generally they work for the

> I believe, by the way, that the CFP® designation should be a mandatory prerequisite for anyone dealing with clients' money in any capacity as a financial advisor.

big bank-owned firms in a culture focused on transactional selling of stocks and bonds. Analysts help them to determine the most attractive current securities, and that's what they sell. They are not financial planners or retirement income planners. They are salespeople. They know how to sell stuff, make money for the bank, and earn commissions, but they don't know how to create lifelong sustainable income streams for their clients.

They Don't Want To Do Financial Planning

Alright, I know many financial advisors will take issue with this particular excuse. They will say their job is to manage money – period. They are not financial planners nor do they want to be. The fact is, though, that at this stage of life their clients really need a plan. You can't simply continue buying and selling stuff inside a vacuum when clients rely on an income from their assets. Without the bigger story – how much income a client needs, where to get it, what other sources of guaranteed income the client has and how taxation will affect the income stream – it's impossible to provide adequate advice.

Becoming a planner pushes these advisors out of their comfort zone of what they know. Planning is a whole different discipline, and it requires a completely different set of skills and training. Most traditional advisors simply don't want to learn these skills: they would rather just buy and sell stuff for clients. For those who might consider this avenue and become a financial planner, they really should become a CERTIFIED FINANCIAL PLANNER® - CFP®, because it is the most comprehensive professional designation available. But this takes considerable time, effort and money. (I believe, by the way, that the CFP® designation should be a mandatory prerequisite for anyone dealing with clients' money in any capacity as a financial advisor.)

Once again, if a broker or financial advisor doesn't want to do his job within the context of financial planning, that's OK. But he shouldn't work with those clients who will rely on his expertise to help ensure their nest egg lasts for the rest of their life while providing an income along the way. He should focus instead on the clients who are still accumulating their wealth and who have the time to recover from a correction that wipes out 30% or more of their portfolio.

They Don't Have the Time

This is one of those excuses that can be used by anyone for just about anything. Some financial advisors point the finger of blame at industry regulators, who are burying them with compliance paperwork. It's true that the industry's onerous compliance rules require more time, but this is not a legitimate excuse. Other industries face the same challenge, and they find ways to deal with it. Sadly, in the financial services industry, far too many advisors don't treat what they do as a professional business. If they did, they'd acknowledge the need for a support structure that allows them to focus on the most important element of their business – the client. By putting the client first, they would then be able to take the time required to learn everything they could about how to switch gears from the old accumulation model to the retirement income model.

They Wont' Make The Effort

Not only does major change take time, it also takes considerable effort. Many advisors are simply unwilling to do the work required for such a fundamental change in their business model. To make this adjustment they have to address a number of areas. They have to research the different kinds of products required to provide income rather than growth. Some of these products, like annuities and variable annuities, require a different license. If the advisor doesn't hold an insurance license, he will have to get one, and this will require effort to study and write a couple of exams. If he doesn't want to do that, then he may have to form a partnership with an insurance licensed advisor, which also takes time and energy.

He has to revamp his business processes and administrative systems. Together with his staff, the advisor will have to develop new processes and procedures. He will also have to learn all the administrative requirements for the new products he'll be dealing with. For many advisors the adjustment requires far too much effort for the potential payoff, and so they simply won't make it.

They Don't Get Paid As Much

The buck stops here, as another saying goes, which applies to this last excuse. It's probably the major reason why advisors won't change how they manage their clients' money. Unfortunately, many advisors place their compensation before the best interests of their client. In fact, this is a very common topic under discussion on financial blogs.

Having seen many clients' statements over the years from accounts that other advisors manage, I have concrete evidence of this tendency. It is sad to say how often I've seen trades executed or products recommended seemingly because of the compensation that they generated for the advisor. I've seen churning, as well, where new investments are recommended solely based on the timing of a deferred sales charge schedule. When the deferred sales charge expires, the advisor recommends selling the investment and buying another one so that he can start getting paid again.

A lot of the time, though, the problem isn't based on what the client has been sold, it's more about what the client hasn't been sold. Many income-generating products that should be in a client's portfolio simply aren't there. Some clients need fixed income investments in their retirement account to provide a minimum income payment each year. No matter what happens in the market, this part of the portfolio won't be affected, and the income will remain rock solid. The investment might be a GIC, CD, a bond, a money market account, a cash account, an annuity or even a solid dividend-paying stock or mutual fund.

But they aren't there. Why? The reason is pretty clear. Advisors aren't paid as much on these types of investments. The advisor may try to justify this by saying these types of investment don't generate sufficient returns, that it has nothing to do with the commission. Let's not forget, though, that, when a client has entered the spending phase for her investments, the goal is less about maximizing return and more about generating a sustainable income. And that is why fixed income should be used, regardless of how that might affect the advisor's paycheque.

All of these excuses are unacceptable. An advisor who manages money for retired clients who need income from their investments had better learn how to do it properly. If he doesn't, then perhaps it is time for the advisor to retire himself.

Chapter 5: An industry at fault

In the last chapter, I discussed the potential risk to your retirement dreams from financial advisors and brokers who still focus on wealth accumulation strategies and who haven't made the transition to retirement income planning. There are some really good retirement income planning specialists, but they are few and far between.

The need for retirement income planning didn't pop up out of nowhere. People have required this kind of planning for decades. It has become more prevalent lately because of the number of boomers preparing to retire over the coming decade or two. These boomers have amassed more wealth, are living longer and are more active than previous generations of retirees, and they have many more options available. This increases the complexity of their financial situation and requires professional guidance.

Considering the large number of people who need this type of planning, a fundamental shift will have to occur in the way industry participants meet their needs. No doubt, this generation has the power to force such changes. They've done it in many other industries on their journey from babies to retiring boomers. To date, however, the financial services industry has given only lip service to this issue and has not made any significant changes. In particular, the industry has done very little to facilitate financial advisors' transition to retirement income planning. There has been lots of talk but very little concrete action.

There are a few specific reasons why the industry has been so slow and reluctant to change. But before I discuss them, you should understand what I mean when I say "the financial services industry." I'm referring to banks, credit unions, brokerages, mutual fund companies, insurance companies, managing general agencies, mutual fund dealers and any other company or institution that deals directly with the public and promotes and sells any type of financial product.

The Cards Are Stacked Against You

We must face one undeniable truth regarding the financial services industry. Financial companies are in the business of making a profit. Sure, they all say they are in business to serve the client. To a degree, that's true. Without clients there is no financial services industry and no companies within that industry. And don't get me wrong. We need profitable businesses to make a free economy work. That is not at issue here. But anyone who has worked long enough inside the industry can see its true motive – profit for shareholders. In some countries like Canada, you've done well if you've owned shares in some of these companies, either directly or indirectly through mutual funds or segregated funds.

Over the course of the financial meltdown of 2008, however, it became painfully obvious that some companies' quest for the almighty profit completely overrode their responsibility for the best interest of their clients.

At the end of the day, the industry has made little progress in properly addressing the needs of retiring boomers. Granted, it has developed some very complex new products like Guaranteed Minimum Withdrawal Benefit plans (GMWBs) and some other obscure product offerings. These have been introduced with significant hype and fanfare, seemingly as an attempt by the industry to address the growing income needs of retiring clients.

But products by themselves are not the answer. The industry needs to address and fix much deeper structural problems first. Until this happens it can pump out as many new product innovations as it can dream up, but they won't address the real problems or provide help to people who need it most.

Captive Sales Force and Tied Selling:

Many of the investment products in Canada today are sold through a captive sales force at major financial institutions. At these firms financial planning or wealth management divisions give the appearance of providing comprehensive advice. Most of them attempt to diversify their offerings beyond their own proprietary products, but the attempt is largely window dressing. For the most part, these captive sales forces sell nothing but their own in-house products. Why shouldn't they? That's where the maximum profit lies.

The real problem here is that retiring boomers need a different type of service that includes independent advice and a diversity of product offerings. These major players either can't offer such service, because of regulations, or don't want to offer it. Obviously their advice can't be independent if it's tied to their own products.

To further compound the problem, there are some very good people working at these institutions, their clients like and trust them and that's a good thing. But they're handcuffed to a limited suite of solutions. In a business built more on relationships and trust than money, these trusted advisors, who want to do the best job they can for their clients, must sell a restricted range of products to keep their jobs, regardless of whether or not a product is truly the best solution for the client.

I know this from first- hand experience. Back in 2003 when I began to see the need to transform my business model to retirement income planning, I worked at one of these firms as part of their so-called captive sales force. I was creating some very comprehensive financial plans and won a national financial planning award from an industry group outside of the company that I represented. But I had a real problem. I was unable to implement some of the solutions for my clients simply because the products were not on my authorized product shelf. So I had to make a choice. I could either try to fit a square peg into a round hole and hope that it would work out for my clients or I could leave the organization and find a place to apply my craft where all the product options were available.

I chose to leave that captive sales force to become an independent advisor. As an independent financial planner and advisor, I could finally create and implement plans with the appropriate solutions. In the future, boomers who need comprehensive plans for retirement income and asset preservation needs will obtain them from this type of advisor.

Part Timers

Some companies with captive sales forces employ part-time advisors. They don't always hire them part-time, but many advisors end up putting in only a part-time effort. These companies hire advisors on contract. They are self employed, which means they are in control of their own hours. For a variety of reasons, many end up working part-time, which doesn't always address the best interests of their clients. Even worse, at least one company in Canada and the U.S. recruits its advisors through network marketing. It focuses on attracting people who want to earn a bit of extra income on the side. This arrangement may work for companies that sell laundry soap, vitamins or Tupperware, but it doesn't work when it involves a client's financial future.

Fragmented Regulatory Framework

Regulation of the financial services industry has not made enough progress to properly address the changing needs of boomers. It remains incredibly fragmented and complex. In Canada, there are different regulators for investment activities and insurance advisors. Banks, meanwhile, are regulated nationally under the federal Bank Act. There is no single national securities regulator to oversee all those who sell investment products. There have been a number of attempts to create one, but each has failed. The job is left to each individual province and territory.

In the life insurance industry in Canada since the 1980's insurance agents must work through a Managing General Agent, rather than dealing directly with the insurance companies. All life insurance business including insurance based investments must flow through an MGA. The problem is MGA's are completely unregulated.

Today as I write this book, the federal government's attempt to bring together the competing regional regulators to form a national securities regulator was struck down by the Supreme Court of Canada as unconstitutional.

The closest Canada has come to a nationally regulated securities industry has been the creation of the Canadian Securities Administrators (CSA). This is an **informal body, with voluntary participation** from all 10 provinces and 3 territories. Their stated mandate is to "protect Canadian investors from unfair, improper or fraudulent practices and foster fair and efficient capital markets". Furthermore they are trying to "develop a harmonized approach to securities regulation in Canada".

One must keep in mind this organization is not a "legislated body" and has no powers as such. It is a collection of participants that have come together to share ideas and try to streamline securities regulation in Canada. They do provide some valuable resources to the investing public, yet because of its voluntary nature, it is not as effective as it could be. The CSA does provide information in 4 key areas for the investing public:

1. A registration database of approved persons across Canada (strangely with the exception of Ontario and Quebec)

2. An Enforcement Database of "disciplined persons" across Canada

3. A Cease Trade Orders Database for companies and individuals across Canada

4. Education tools for the individual investor

I'll provide more information on how you can use these tools created by the CSA later in the book.

If this isn't complicated enough, another layer of quasi-regulation exists in Canada called self-regulatory organizations or SROs. As the name implies, these organizations have been set up to police their own members. There are two main SRO's in Canada for the investment industry. The Mutual Fund Dealers Association of Canada (MFDA) was established for advisors who only sell mutual funds. The Investment Industry Regulatory Organization of Canada (IIROC) is for advisors who sell mutual funds as well as a wide range of other securities.

These organizations, while well-intentioned, were never designed to ensure that clients get the type or quality of planning advice they need. Their basic mandate is to ensure investment suitability in line with client's individual circumstances. That is to say, making sure that investments recommended by advisors are in line with the client's objectives, time horizon and the level of risk they are willing to take. Even so, these SRO's have been unable to completely protect clients from unethical advisors, especially those who are not regulated. Also, these organizations are funded by the members whom they regulate. This in itself presents an interesting conflict of interest.

The result of all of this fragmentation is that there is no cohesive regulation to protect or treat consumers equally. A rule that applies in B.C. may not apply in Ontario or Nova Scotia. And as boundaries disappear between insurance companies and traditional investment companies, there is increased confusion as to who is supposed to be regulating whom. For instance, who should be regulating a segregated fund sold through an insurance company when the underlying investment is actually managed by a mutual fund company? And what about the advisor who sells that segregated fund? Until this gets sorted out, territorial arguments will continue between the various regulators, and they will not be focusing on what really matters – protecting clients' interests and ensuring they receive the best possible advice.

A Case Study in Futility

Let's assume there's a "hypothetical" advisor in Ontario who is investigated by the MFDA. It turns out that he had clearly broken a number of MFDA rules and put clients in jeopardy. As a result the MFDA decides to impose a significant fine and ban him for life from holding a Mutual Funds License. Coincidently, around the same time the Ontario Securities Commission (OSC) began investigating this same advisor for another serious, yet unrelated infraction. The OSC also decided to ban this advisor from holding a securities license for life. Sounds like justice was served and clients were protected, right?

> **The result of all of this fragmentation is that there is no cohesive regulation to protect or treat consumers equally.**

Not so fast. Here's how the rest of the story might unfold. Even though the MFDA and the OSC could ban this advisor for life from holding a securities or mutual funds license he could continue in business selling investments that are not regulated by either the MFDA or OSC. As for the fine, the MFDA can levy one, but has no legislated authority to collect it.

To make matters worse, let's assume this advisor was also licensed to sell insurance products, including segregated funds, which he sells through an unregulated MGA. Because that license falls under the Financial Services Commission of Ontario (FSCO) his insurance business would be unaffected by the bans from the MFDA and OSC. You see FSCO isn't concerned about an advisor's exploits outside of its jurisdiction.

The bottom line:

Without a national coordinated securities regulator, covering all types of investments, an advisor could be banned for life from the securities side of the business, and yet continue selling investments on the insurance side of the business through a managing general agency. And because so many insurance companies have partnered with mutual fund companies, he is in essence quite likely able to sell some of the same mutual funds, he was banned from selling directly. The only difference is they are now wrapped inside of a segregated fund. How's that for protecting the client?

Part 2
Solutions

Chapter 6: Investment projections are not retirement income plans

If you stopped reading this book right now, you'd likely think that your golden years will be anything but golden. I have to admit that the first half of the book was a little depressing to write. But these are the realities that boomers including myself are going to face. And what about that story at the beginning of the book about finding and spending the pot of gold at the end of the rainbow? When will we get to that? Very soon, I promise.

In my financial planning practice I have always been a realist and have tried to tell it like it is when reviewing my clients' financial lives. For the most part, people appreciate this straightforward approach. One of the fundamentals of creating a rock-solid retirement income plan is to know where you're starting from and identify the things that may pop up in the future that could derail your best-laid plans.

That's why I spent so much time on this in the first half of the book. You need to know the issues. Only then can you address them so you can live a worry-free retirement. You need to know that you've identified the potential problems and that your plan puts solutions in place to deal with them.

With a proper retirement income plan, based on time-proven principles, the money side of retirement is the easy part. Figuring out what you'll do with your time may ultimately end up being more difficult.

What is a Retirement Income Plan?

Many people have been misled about the definition of a retirement income plan. Let's start by talking about what it's not. It isn't a retirement investment portfolio. It isn't a GIC, a CD, a Stock, a Bond, a RRIF, or a 401K. These are products, not plans. Products will be part of the plan, but they are not a plan by themselves.

Nor is a plan an investment projection. I can't tell you how many times over the years I've asked prospective clients to bring along their financial or retirement plan when we first meet, only to have them bring in a simple investment projection. They're not to blame for this mistake, by the way. In all my years in this business, I've only ever seen two financial plans written by other advisors.

An investment projection is a printout from a bank or broker that shows how your investment portfolio (stock, bond, mutual fund, GIC or CD etc) will grow or decline over time, assuming a certain rate of interest or growth and accounting for any income that you may withdraw. For Canadians reading this book, a RRIF projection also doesn't count as a retirement plan. All that shows is how long your RRIF account will last, assuming a certain rate of return, relative to the prescribed amount of income you must take out of the RRIF account each year. Such projections will be used when creating a complete retirement income plan, but they only make up a small part of the overall plan.

Retirement Income Plan - Defined

A retirement income plan in its most basic form is a simple listing of all the possible sources of income that you can expect to receive in retirement. This would include things like: government pensions (CPP, OAS and Social Security in the USA), company pension(s), private annuities, rental income, royalties, and business income that may continue into retirement. The list should also include projected income from investment accounts – both taxable (non-registered) and retirement accounts (RRSP, RRIF, TFSA, 401k etc).

At this point, investment projections may become confused with retirement plans. In fact, your list should include any and all sources of income.

For some people, simply knowing how much income they can expect to receive becomes their plan. They will just spend what they get.

A more advanced and useful retirement income plan also addresses the other side of the picture – your expenses. It's useful to know how much income you can expect when you retire. It's even more useful to know if your savings will generate enough income to cover your expenses for the rest of your life. You can determine this only by addressing the expense side of the equation. *For people approaching retirement, not knowing if their income will cover their expenses presents a major cause of anxiety.*

> For people approaching retirement, not knowing if their income will cover their expenses presents a major cause of anxiety.

Unlike an investment projection, a **retirement income plan** is a written document that shows in black and white how your income will cover all your expenses during retirement. Expenses include the obvious ones like food and utility bills. They also include taxes and inflation. If your income doesn't cover all your expenses, your plan will quantify the shortfall so that you can take steps to address it. Your plan will also show you how to position your investments and savings to produce the income you'll need to cover your expenses. A retirement income plan can be as simple as a Word document that summarizes your income and expenses or as complex as a report prepared by a financial advisor using advanced financial planning software. The point is, you need a plan.

Now that we've cleared that up, let's get on to learning how to generate a worry-free life-long income. This stuff isn't rocket science. It may even seem simplistic. But sometimes the simplest solutions are the best solutions.

As for that pot of gold, the rest of this book will focus on solutions, and how to create your own retirement income plan. By using this information and implementing a plan, your pot of gold will be better protected and will provide you with the income you need to do all the things that are important to you. At the end of the day, isn't that what you want? That's what my clients keep telling me. In fact, here's what Jack and Jill (not their real names) said in a recent letter to me after their retirement income plan allowed them to retire:

Chapter 6: Investment projections are not retirement income plans   65

"When we first met you, we were working with a broker at a major financial institution and were considering our options about how and when to retire. At that time we asked for some guidance with this major life transition, but all we were given was a booklet to fill out and told to return it, and someone we didn't even know would create a plan for us. That's when we started working with you. You were willing to spend whatever time was needed with us to get to really know and understand our situation. Not only that, you kept things simple and understandable, which always gives us comfort in your recommendations. We don't believe that we would have been able to retire when we did if it had not been for the financial plan you created for us. We simply would not have had the confidence to do so without it."

Here's what you'll learn in the next few chapters. In chapter 7, I'll introduce you to a simple concept called the Four Planning Cornerstones. You can use this concept to create a basic plan for yourself.

In chapters 8 and 9, I reveal the secrets of my retirement income planning system called **The Fearless Retirement Blueprint.** I use this system to create lifelong income for clients so they can enjoy retirement without financial worry. In chapter 8, I'll teach you how to match your spending to your sources of income during retirement. You'll learn to divide your big pot of gold into a number of smaller pots and match them directly to your spending needs. In the process, you'll determine if your expenses will exceed your guaranteed sources of income. It's critical that you identify this gap before you create your plan.

In chapter 9, I'll reveal a strategy called product allocation that you can use to fill the gap.

With these two concepts, you'll have the basic building blocks to create an income that will last your lifetime.

Once you understand this you can create your own plan. That's the focus of chapter 13 where you can roll up your sleeves to create your own plan if you wish.

If you would rather hire a professional planner to do it for you, I'll help you to find the right one in chapters 10, 11 and 12. After reading about financial-advisor risk and the faults of the industry, you may wonder where to begin. These three chapters will show you.

I'll begin in chapter 10 by showing you how to avoid hiring a thief like Bernie Madoff, who stole billions of dollars from good hard-working people like you. I'll explain how to conduct some basic research so you can compile a thorough reference check on a prospective advisor.

In chapter 11, I'll pull back the curtains on the industry to demystify the way advisors get paid through the different fees that they charge. Most people have no idea how their advisor gets paid. This can lead to another form of client abuse. A little bit of knowledge may save you a lot of money.

Finally, in chapter 12, I'll address the basics of choosing an advisor. I'll show you how to determine if an advisor is planning-focused or transaction-focused. I'll also show you how to interview a few prospects to make sure they're planning-focused.

Alright, let's get started with the Four Planning Cornerstones.

Chapter 7: The four planning cornerstones

Earlier I said, "The money side of retirement is the easy part." Many people, though, especially in the financial services industry, try to make this the complicated part. It doesn't have to be complicated, not if you understand the concepts that I'll show you.

I've used a couple of methods over the years to create plans. The concepts are not new, revolutionary or unique. They are, however, based on common sense and a bit of psychology.

The first is a simple concept called The Four Planning Cornerstones. I'll start with this concept to ease you into the world of planning. Once you see how simple it can be, I'll introduce you to another system that I use for my clients. And I'll teach you how to use it yourself.

The Four Planning Cornerstones

I learned this concept in my early years as an advisor. Initially I used it as a way to help clients structure their overall financial life. It's as effective for people saving for retirement as it is for people entering their retirement. Since you'll use this model for retirement income planning, you'll first have to determine how much income, if any, you need to generate from your savings. We discussed this in the previous chapter. Once you do this, you can easily apply the Four Planning Cornerstones.

Table 6: The Four Planning Cornerstones

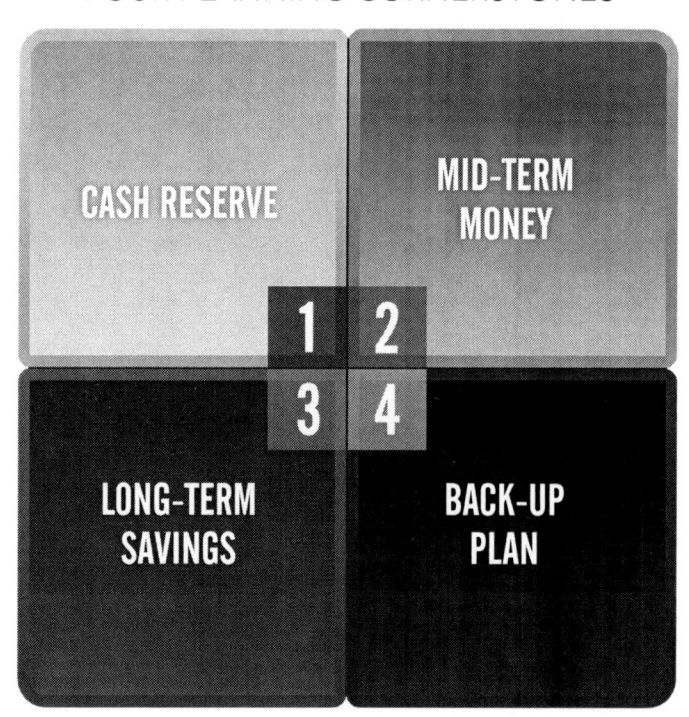

FOUR PLANNING CORNERSTONES

1 CASH RESERVE	**2** MID-TERM MONEY
3 LONG-TERM SAVINGS	**4** BACK-UP PLAN

Like a new home, your financial life needs a strong foundation, or else the rest of the building could tumble down. Table 6 shows the four areas that form the cornerstones of your financial life. To create a solid, well-balanced financial life, you need to set aside some money for each of them.

1. Cash Reserve (aka rainy day account):

Life happens! When it does, it tends to cost money. Whether it's a major home repair that the insurance company won't pay for, or a temporary job loss - we need to pay for stuff. Having money saved and set aside in a cash reserve allows us to get through these times with less stress, because we don't have to figure out where to come up with the money. On the positive side, having a short-term reserve (also called a rainy day account) allows us to take advantage of opportunities when they come up. Perhaps it's a once in a lifetime trip or buying that one-of-a- kind piece of art that came up for auction. Maybe it's the ability to give a little extra to your favorite charity when they need it the most or take the grandkids to Disney World. The point is, when life happens, if we don't have a cash reserve we have to either borrow the money or dip into other investments, perhaps at an inopportune time (like during a market correction).

In the context of a retirement income plan, having a rainy day account is a crucial component. It gives you the ability to do those extra things that come up, without dipping into investments that are set aside to provide ongoing income. People without such an account may think long and hard about accessing investments to pay for that extra trip or to buy that new ride-on lawnmower on sale for 50% off, especially during a market meltdown. Bottom line is a cash reserve gives you flexibility and peace of mind, no matter what's going on in the other areas of your financial life or in the world around you.

How much should you set aside? This amount will be different for everyone. Over the years I've found that the amount is determined more by a feeling of safety and security than by an actual number. One person may feel quite comfortable with $5,000 while another can't sleep without $50,000 sitting in the bank. Your situation is unique, so think about how much ready cash you might need in the next year and set it aside.

2. Mid-Term Money

This is an oft forgotten area of planning, but it plays a vital role, particularly in the spending phase of life. Once you have adequate short-term reserves set up, you should consider setting up some of your money for mid-term goals. This could be considered as anything you may want to do or have to pay for in the next 3-5 years. For some this is making sure there's money set aside for a major vacation, not the regular annual ones. For others, this is the place to park some money for the regular purchase of a new vehicle, assuming you don't finance or lease it.

When it comes to the spending phase of life, mid-term money also forms a key to surviving a market meltdown without worry. The financial markets are totally out of our control, and they tend to move in long-term trends. By their very nature this means they must correct periodically, and this can put your retirement income at risk if all your money is in the market, so to speak. Having a portion of your money in both cash reserves (where money is not at risk) and mid-term money savings (where there is a bit of risk) gives you a chance to get through even a major correction.

The engine that drives your retirement income will be the money in your long-term savings/investments. But when the market corrects, the value of this pot of money will no doubt go down, sometimes substantially. This is where people begin to have problems and the worry starts to set in. When the market goes down our expenses don't usually change. As a result someone in this situation could be forced to take the same income from a smaller asset (which over time compounds the problem). Or they're forced to take a smaller income.

> Life happens! When it does, it tends to cost money.

To avoid this scenario, if you have a cash reserve, you could supplement your income from there. If the correction in the market lasts for a year or more, then having access to mid-term money to supplement your income is another great alternative. This will allow your long-term assets to grow again as the markets recover.

How much should you set aside as mid-term money? Again, individuals make their own decisions based on each of their unique situations. Start by giving some thought to any projects, extended trips or purchases you've planned over the next few years. Figure out how much they'll likely cost, and set aside that amount in a mid-term investment.

If you're drawing income from your long-term assets, you might set aside enough mid-term money to cover one to two years of income payments. When the next market correction comes, you'll have enough income to keep you going for one to two years, and you won't have to worry when the markets don't bounce right back.

3. Long-Term Savings

This section should be very familiar to those of you who have saved money throughout your life for retirement. While accumulating your nest egg, long-term savings is that part of your financial plan where you designate funds for your future. Long-term is generally considered to be anything over 10 years in the future. So generally this money is to be used to help provide an income once you're no longer working. But it could be for any other financial goal that's quite far out in the future. For instance, some consider a child's education as a long-term goal worth saving for.

This area is important for the simple fact that, if you don't put aside some money for the future, you'll likely have some financial difficulties once you no longer receive a paycheque from work. You may end up having to work longer, significantly adjust your lifestyle in retirement or maybe even sell your home before you want to. Over the years, I've heard many people say they want to live for today because they may not even live until retirement. My response to that has always been, "But what if you do live a long healthy life?" There's something to be said about living for today, but I think there needs to be some balance, and hence the use of the Four Planning Cornerstones.

How does this apply to someone who's retired or about to retire? Let's not forget that retirement could last for 30 years. Therefore any long-term savings accumulated over a working life will still be considered long-term savings. It's not like you'll spend it all in the first year of retirement right? The only difference is that now these savings will be used to provide a portion of your overall income, so you'll want to have more of a focus on income generating investments. Naturally there should be a change in how and where those funds are invested, but a long-term focus should still remain as one of the deciding factors.

How much should you keep in long-term savings? The answer will depend on a number of factors, including how much you've set aside for short-term and mid-term purposes. Keep in mind that this part of your savings will provide your ongoing income.

As I mentioned, you should set aside enough mid-term money to cover one to two years of income to protect yourself against major market corrections. If you draw income from your mid-term money, you should refill the pot each year to maintain the buffer. This is where your long-term savings can help. You simply set up a portion of your long-term money so that it generates enough annual income to replace the mid-term money that you take as income. If you take $12,000 from your mid-term savings, you should replace the money with $12,000 generated by your long-term savings. You can let the rest of your long-term savings grow as a way to keep up with inflation or to cover future long-term health care costs if you haven't purchased insurance for that purpose.

4. Back-Up Plan (aka insurance):

We've already talked about how life happens, and sometimes bad things happen to good people. Unfortunately this can mean that people have to endure substantial financial hardship, if they haven't taken steps to protect themselves.

What we are really talking about in this cornerstone is insurance. I know, I know. If you're like most people you despise insurance, and justifiably so, I might add. Having worked in the industry, and having seen some of the sales tactics and salespeople, I don't really blame you. But the truth of the matter is insurance should be a very important part of everyone's financial life. If used properly, it can protect us and our families from the unexpected. The problem with insurance isn't so much the product but in how it's sold. But that's a whole other topic for another book.

While we're on our journey to amass this pot of gold for the future, there are two things that we need to protect. One is the wealth we've been building (assets) and the second is our income. Without our ability to earn an income, we can no longer contribute money to build our assets for the future. And if we die along the way before the plan is fully funded, it may simply fall apart. This is where life and disability insurance come into the picture.

If we get sick or injured, disability and critical illness insurance is there to provide an income while we can't work, so our bills get paid and we won't be forced to dip into our long-term savings. On the other hand, dying can also have a devastating effect on our family's finances. Life insurance is a simple, inexpensive tool that can be used to eliminate the financial hardship placed on a family when one or both of the income earners dies. Insurance proceeds are a great way to pay off debts and to provide an ongoing income for the surviving family members. This will allow for the assets (like savings and even the house) to be preserved for the future we'd envisioned.

That's great for those who are still in the saving phase of life, but what about those who have now entered the spending stage? What income and assets do they need to protect? There's no question that the situation is different at this stage of life. What I often say to clients is: at this stage of life insurance becomes more of a want than a need. There's still income to protect as well as assets, but the reason for protection is different. Let me explain, using my situation as an example.

Right now I have a young family that depends on me for support. If I can't earn a living because I'm disabled or dead, there will be a problem paying for my family's lifestyle. So at this stage of my life, I have a pure need for insurance to ensure my family members have a roof over their heads, can still eat, pay the bills and afford to go to university. Once my kids are grown and I don't have any debts, this pure need disappears. However, I may continue to want insurance for estate planning purposes. In my case, I might want to make sure my estate was maximized by limiting the effects of taxes on my death. This is where I could use permanent life insurance.

As for protecting income during retirement, there may not be the same pure need as when you're working. However, there may be a desire to ensure that a certain minimum level of income is guaranteed. It might be to cover your basic expenses, or to protect against market downturns, inflation, low interest rates or the costs of future long-term care. Once again, insurance can play a key role here, but a different kind of insurance. The two kinds of insurance I'm referring to are: long-term care insurance and insurance attached to certain types of retirement income products. These types of insurance may not be familiar to you. For an explanation of both please see the appendix.

How do you set aside money for this cornerstone? In this case you aren't generally going to set aside any lump sums of money. It's more about deciding that you want to share the costs of certain risks, by purchasing insurance. That said if you decide this is something you want to do then you'll be paying additional money as an expense in the form of an insurance premium. In the case of long term care insurance you'll have to budget for the premium to be paid monthly or annually out of your cash flow. This may mean having to take additional income from your investments. For an alternative solution to paying for long term care insurance, check out the case study in Appendix #1.

When it comes to insurance on retirement income products like a Guaranteed Living Income Benefit plan, the cost of that type of insurance is built into the product in the form of additional management fees. As such you won't have a direct expense to pay, but it will cost you in the increased fees.

A history lesson you can apply in the future.

To see how the Four Planning Cornerstone approach can really work, let's look at a recent example where it wasn't used. You'll see the very negative impact that not having such a plan, had on the lives of many retirees.

During the market meltdown of 2008 all the major stock markets around the globe gave back more than 30% of their value. At that time I met many people through my seminars and TV show, and the financial losses I saw were staggering. Not to mention the significant negative impact it had on their incomes. They were also quite unnecessary.

I can't imagine how many people could have avoided these huge losses, along with the concern, fear and anger that came with the experience, had they, or more importantly, their advisors applied the Four Planning Cornerstones to create a retirement income plan.

During the height of the meltdown stories in the media proliferated about retirees' investment portfolios being devastated (some were reportedly down more than 50%). People had to go back to work just to make ends meet. Others who couldn't go back to work had to make substantial changes to their spending just to survive, or even worse go into debt. Proof of this was seen in an increase in advertising for reverse mortgages. Reverse mortgages at the best of times are a very poor financial strategy. As a last resort in a market crisis, they should be used only under significant duress.

Why were so many people affected in such a negative way by the meltdown? The simple truth is that most folks didn't have a retirement income plan, and they quite likely had most, if not all, of their money in one area – the long-term savings pot. They had no significant cash reserve to help weather the storm. There was no mid-term money to help support their lifestyle while they waited for the markets to come back over the next couple of years (as they always do). And they

> I can't imagine how many people could have avoided these huge losses, along with the concern, fear and anger that came with the experience, had they, or more importantly, their advisors applied the Four Planning Cornerstones to create a retirement income plan.

probably chose not to pay extra fees on guaranteed income products prior to the meltdown because they were convinced that these "high fees" weren't worth it. Maybe they didn't even know about such guaranteed income products, or worse, maybe their advisors weren't aware of them or simply didn't offer them. The old saying, that hindsight is 20/20, surely fits this situation.

If If nothing else this example illustrates how using the Four Planning Cornerstones to create a plan can help avoid major financial stress and hardship, whenever a major market correction happens.

So that's the Four Planning Cornerstones. This simple concept will work whether you're in the accumulation phase before retirement or the next stage of life. It's really about splitting up your money into a few different pots, each one having its own separate purpose. Come to think of it, this is really a variation of the old adage - Don't put all your eggs in one basket. The overall advantage being that you'll never have to worry about money, no matter what life throws at you.

Exactly how much should you put into each pot when you reach retirement? That depends on your individual situation. In the next chapter, I'm going to discuss some of the psychology behind retirement income planning and reveal the first secret to my retirement income planning system.

Chapter 8: The psychology of retirement income planning

Now for something a little different and perhaps a bit advanced. Don't worry, when I say advanced I don't mean something so complex that you'll need an engineering degree to understand it. The advanced part of this has to do with understanding a bit of psychology that's behind a relatively simple strategy I'm about to reveal to you. It may seem strange to some people that I would combine the topics of money and psychology. It's almost as taboo as combining religion and politics. My hope, though, is that by the time you finish this chapter you'll see how naturally the two fit together.

Before I get to the nuts and bolts of this section, I want to share a bit of my story with you. The purpose is to show you how certain events changed my life so I could positively affect the lives of others, as they relate to retirement planning.

When I was applying for university, I thought my calling was economics. I worked very hard and got accepted to my school of choice to study economics in the spring of 1985.

Life has a funny way of taking us in different directions than the ones we think we should be going, though. For me, this new path started when tragedy struck my family. In the final months of high school, my father died suddenly of a heart attack at age 57. Here I was, 18 years old, about to embark on a major life challenge, and my world was turned completely upside down. For the first time in my young life, I was facing a new, very real fear of not being safe and secure.

As if that wasn't enough for an 18-year-old to deal with, within 3 weeks of my father's passing, I had a near death experience of my own. I was going to school one morning on my motorcycle, as I did every morning. But this particular morning, out of nowhere, a car pulled out in front of me from a side street. In that moment, my life could have ended. Somehow, though, I managed to veer right, avoiding a head-on collision with the car and a transport truck. I didn't miss the car completely, though. I hit the rear wheel on the driver's side at roughly 65 km/hour. This brought my motorcycle to an instant stop. For me, Newton's law of inertia still applied and I continued through the air, landing roughly 25 feet from the crash. Miraculously, I escaped serious injury. No broken bones, no burned off skin, just some bumps and bruises. My bike, on the other hand was a total write off.

There are a couple of things I will never forget from that moment. The first is how fast it happened, all within a split second. The other is the comment from the ambulance attendants who responded to the accident. I was sitting on a curb at the side of the road when they arrived. They got out, looked at the bike, looked at the car and said, "Where's the driver of the bike? With this mess, there's no way he could have walked away". But there I was, sitting relatively unscathed.

After the accident, the logical side of my brain gave credit for surviving to my defensive driving skills. My parents, in their wisdom (although I didn't see it that way at the time), had insisted on my taking a defensive driving course for motorcycles at the local college as a condition of getting my bike license. In that course, we learned how to make split-second decisions, to constantly scan our surroundings for danger and a way out if something happened. We also learned how to fall off our bikes by crashing them into bales of hay. The natural and logical conclusion for me at the time was that I'd learned what I needed in that course and that's how I survived the crash.

Upon reflection over the years, I now believe there was something else at play on that morning in June of 1985. Some would say it was fate or destiny. Others may say I had a guardian angel looking over me. I believe it was fate, and that the guardian angel was my father. I think he reached down, grabbed me off the bike and set me down out of harm's way. Those who don't believe in such things will say this is silly talk. But to me, those events somehow reshaped the path my life ultimately took, and there had to be a reason.

When I got to university a few short months later to begin in the economics program, something had changed for me. I'd worked hard to qualify academically for this difficult program, yet for reasons unknown to me, I no longer had any desire to take economics. Looking back, it almost seems irrational now, but I did the unthinkable: I changed my major that first week from economics to psychology.

You're probably wondering why I'm telling you this and what it has to do with building a lifelong income that you can't outlive. This story lays the foundation for my introduction to the discipline of psychology, even though it would take years and a couple of career changes before I saw the connection to retirement income planning. It was during my time at Wilfrid Laurier University, while studying psychology that I first learned about Maslow's Hierarchy of Needs. We'll come back to that later. And while I didn't know it at the time, this was the starting point for my lifelong journey in a career focused on helping people live safe and financially secure lives.

> Your financial plan and the relationship you have with your advisor have more to do with your motivations, hopes, dreams and fears than about the money.

Even in the early days of my career as a financial planner, I talked to clients about how money by itself isn't important. In fact, I've been known to say that money by itself is boring, especially in the modern world, where we don't even get to hold much of it in our hands. Our money has just become numbers in a computer. I've also said that the important thing is what money can do. This concept eventually became the basis for part of the tagline on my TV show: "*Without a plan, it's only money*".

At the end of the day, this all boils down to the fact that your financial plan and the relationship you have with your advisor have more to do with your motivations, hopes, dreams and fears than about the money. No doubt the money is important, but only as a secondary concern. Without this understanding, which is rooted in psychology, you may never have a plan that makes sense for you. I'm certainly not saying that you or your advisor needs to be a psychologist, but some basic understanding of how money relates to your needs and behaviors is crucial. In some way, back in the spring of 1985, my life was altered so that I'd be able to understand eventually this connection and bring the message to many others.

Maslow and his Hierarchy

Who is Maslow, and what is his hierarchy all about? Abraham Maslow was a psychologist who wrote a paper in 1943 called A Theory of Human Motivation. In that paper, he introduced a concept he called A Hierarchy of Needs, through which he suggested that people are motivated to first fulfill certain basic needs before moving on to other needs.

> "Maslow's hierarchy of needs is most often displayed as a pyramid," says writer Kendra van Wagner, "with the lowest levels of the pyramid made up of the most basic needs and the more complex needs at the top of the pyramid. Needs at the bottom of the pyramid are basic physical requirements including the need for food, water, sleep and warmth. Once these lower-level needs have been met, people can move on to the next level of needs, which are for safety and security".[*]

---

[*] From an article on About.com: Psychology, entitled Hierarch of Needs The five levels of Maslow's Hierarchy of Needs, written by Kendra Van Wagner

The Five Levels of Maslow's Hierarchy of Needs:

1. **Physiological Needs**
   These needs are the most basic needs and are considered to be vital to ones survival. They include the need for: water, air, food, sex, sleep and warmth. Maslow postulated that until these needs are met all other needs are essentially unimportant.

2. **Security Needs**
   Moving up the pyramid, once the physiological needs have been met, the next most important needs are for our safety and security. Security needs are also important for our survival, but Maslow's theory suggests that while this is true, they are not as important as our basic physiological needs. Examples would include: shelter from the environment, living in safe neighborhoods, having steady employment, and having health insurance.

3. **Social Needs**
   Such needs include our need to belong, to love and be loved, acceptance by others and affection. To fulfill these needs, we become involved in relationships with family, friends, work colleagues, community organizations, religious groups or romantic partners. Of course, these needs are less basic than both our security and physiological needs.

4. **Esteem Needs**
   Second from the top on the pyramid are esteem needs. These needs reflect our self-esteem or feelings of personal worth, a desire for social recognition and accomplishment.

5. **Self-Actualization**
   At the top of the pyramid we find the need for something Maslow called "self-actualization". After a person has satisfied all the lower needs on the pyramid, Maslow believed that a self-actualized person has become self-aware. This person is now free to focus on personal growth and on achieving what he sees as his full potential.

Maslow and Money

The thing about Maslow and his hierarchy is this: We as humans have certain needs that must be met for us to survive. Once we've met those needs, we move up the pyramid to meet our other needs.

There have certainly been some critics of Maslow's work, but I for one think he is on to something, especially when you relate it to our money needs. If you think about it for a moment, our lives pretty much work the way he has described. Quite simply, we come into this world as babies and require food, water, and warmth to survive. Then we require shelter and protection from anything that could harm us.

Very quickly, as we grow, we begin to bond with our parents. Then as we get older, we begin to socialize, make friends and seek attention and acceptance from various groups. All the while, our parents have been providing the basic necessities of life for us, allowing us to concentrate on these other higher needs.

Eventually we move out of our parents' homes and we get jobs to make money. And what's all the money for? It enables us to buy food and provide ourselves with shelter, as well as keep up with our social activities, which of course cost even more money. As we go through our lives and advance in our careers, we try to improve our standard of living, perhaps by getting a bigger or better house. Maybe we move to one in a better neighborhood. We want to buy a newer and possibly better car. And of course we want to amass a certain amount of wealth that we can use when we retire.

All of this is in an attempt to raise our social status or personal self-worth. Finally at the end of our lives, we want to be remembered for something. Many hope to leave a legacy. This doesn't necessarily have to be a monetary one. Most people want to be remembered for something they did or accomplished in life. That in a nutshell is what Maslow's Hierarchy looks like.

Maslow in Action

For years I prepared financial plans by matching a client's income sources to the Four Planning Cornerstones. I did this by using a cash-flow analysis. I determined clients' spending needs for each of the four cornerstones and matched them to their sources of income. In this way, I ensured that we took care of the most important needs first, using the clients' available resources. This involved a lot of technical work. But I don't think it fully addressed my clients' needs from a human perspective.

That changed a few years ago after I attended a training seminar conducted by a mutual fund company that I use for some clients. The presenter talked about different ways to plan for our clients' income needs in retirement. On a screen, he displayed an Income/Expense Hierarchy (see Figure 3). I saw immediately that it was based on Maslow's Hierarchy of Needs.

In the Income/Expense Hierarchy, expenses corresponded to levels of needs in Maslow's model. With the exception of the "estate/legacy expense", it also resembled my Four Planning Cornerstone approach. Unlike my approach, though, the Income/Expense Hierarchy regarded expenses from a motivational or psychological perspective. I'd found the human perspective that I'd been missing.

I found more than that. Here was a simple way to associate the purpose of money with the boring categories of expenses. Now I could help people to see their expenses in distinct categories based on the bigger purpose in their lives. Framing expenses in the context of Maslow's hierarchy gives money that purpose.

There was just one problem. Visually Maslow's hierarchy makes sense when presented as a pyramid. As you satisfy each category of needs, you progress upward. But in reference to the actual flow of money in and out of a bank account, the pyramid analogy doesn't make as much sense.

That's when I flipped the figure upside down and created a funnel. Visually this made more sense. Money comes into the funnel from various sources. It flows out of the funnel to pay expenses. Expenses are defined in categories based on our needs as defined by Maslow. I call this the Retirement Spending Funnel (see Figure 3a).

Once I saw the connection between our needs in life and the use of our money in this adaptation of Maslow's Hierarchy, I knew I'd found a powerful tool for my clients. I didn't create the original structure in figure 3. But I revised it in my own way. It helps me build retirement income plans based on what really matters to people, not just on some boring spreadsheet of numbers.

In the rest of this chapter, I'll explain in detail how to use the Retirement Spending Funnel to match your income and expenses, based on your purpose and what's important to you.

Figure 3

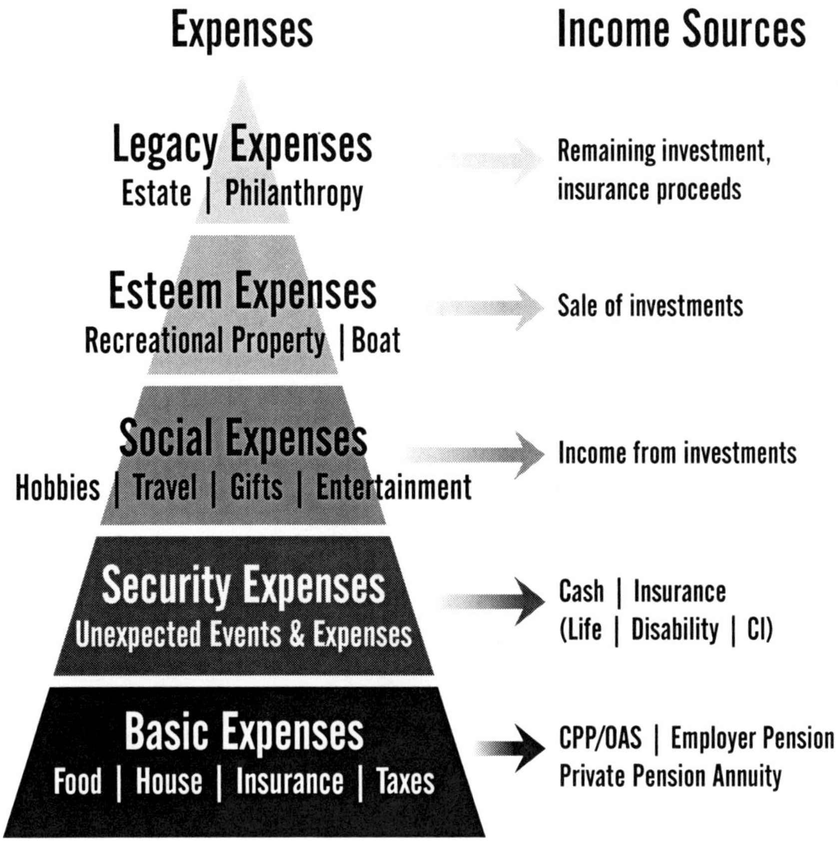
Expenses
Income Sources
Legacy Expenses
Estate | Philanthropy
Remaining investment, insurance proceeds
Esteem Expenses
Recreational Property | Boat
Sale of investments
Social Expenses
Hobbies | Travel | Gifts | Entertainment
Income from investments
Security Expenses
Unexpected Events & Expenses
Cash | Insurance
(Life | Disability | CI)
Basic Expenses
Food | House | Insurance | Taxes
CPP/OAS | Employer Pension
Private Pension Annuity

* **Note**: The original design for this pyramid comes from a presentation by CI Investments in its Advisor Education program.

Figure 3 a RETIREMENT SPENDING FUNNEL

RETIREMENT SPENDING FUNNEL

Funding Categories **Expense Categories** **Gap Analysis**

Guaranteed Income
Government, Work pensions, Annuities → **Basic Expenses** (Food, Gas, Clothing, Shelter, Transportation, Taxes)

Cash, Insurance Premiums (House, Auto Life, Disability, Critical Illness, Long-term Care) → **"What If" Expenses** (Damage, Illness, Injury, etc.)

Non-Guaranteed Income From Investments → **Social Expenses** (Entertainment, Vacations, Sports)

Income Gap Calculator
Guaranteed Income − Expenses = Gap (±)
+ You have an excess income
− You have a gap that needs to be filled

Sale of Investments → **Esteem Expenses** (Luxury Car, Rv, Boat, Exclusive Club Membership)

Final Estate Sale of Investments, Real Estate, Life Insurance Proceeds → **Legacy**

Lump Sum Needs Calculator
Esteem + Legacy = Lump Sum Need

Fearless Retirement Blueprint   Worksheet Series   Financial Doctor Press © 2012

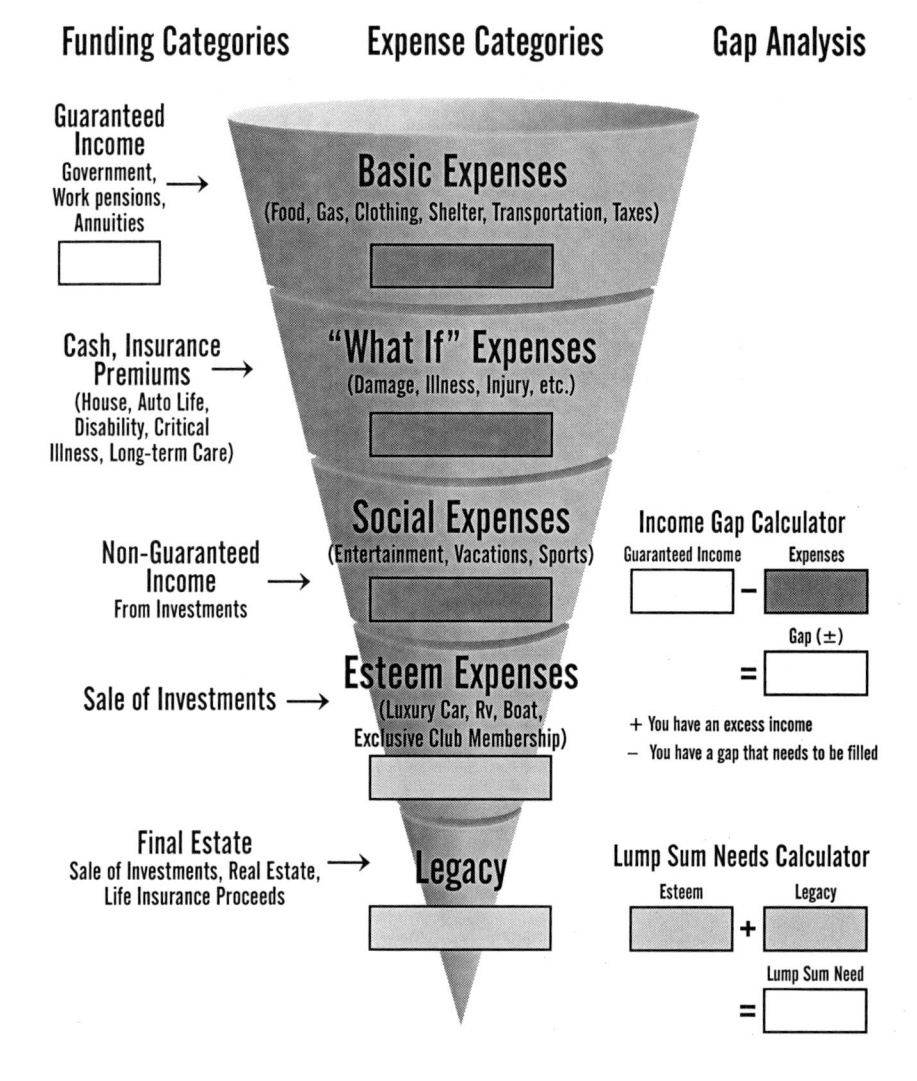

Matching Income and Expenses

Now it's time to get down to business and see how this theory relates to your money. As you can see, there are two distinct sections in Figure 3a. The funnel shows our expense needs according to Maslow's Hierarchy. They're ranked from basic expenses at the top to legacy expenses at the bottom. On the left side of the illustration is a listing of general sources that can be used to fund a particular expense category. Each of these sources matches a need in the funnel. On the right side of the funnel you see a Gap Calculator, and a place to document your total lump sum needs for Esteem and Legacy expenses. You'll learn more about these in an upcoming chapter.

Now I'll take you through the funnel one level at a time and explain how you can use it to cover the expenses you may have in your life. In the appendix of this book, and at www.FearlessRetirementResources.com, you'll find a worksheet that you can use to categorize your income and expenses according to the Retirement Spending Funnel. You'll also find a worksheet to document all of your investment assets that will be available to generate income. You'll need both of these worksheets in Chapter 13 when I show you how to create your own Retirement Income Plan.

Level 1: Basic Expenses

Basic Expenses
(Food, Gas, Clothing, Shelter, Transportation, Taxes)

As with Maslow's Hierarchy of needs, when it comes to our retirement income planning, we want to address our most basic expenses first. These basic expenses are also known as fixed expenses, things we have no choice about paying. As broad categories, this includes things like food, housing, clothing, insurance and taxes. Gone are the days of foraging for our own food and building our own shelters. Today if we want to eat and have some place to live (two things we need to survive), we have to pay for food and lodging. Even though Maslow would likely consider shelter to be a security expense, I've moved it to the basic expense category because in today's society we must live somewhere, and that costs money.

If we look at the food and housing expenses, we can break them down even further to include a whole range of subcategories. Food, for instance, could include groceries as well as eating at restaurants, depending on your lifestyle. Housing includes not only the basic cost of rent or mortgage payments, if you have a mortgage, but also heat, hydro, insurance, maintenance, property taxes etc. Just about anything that costs money and is associated with living in your home should be considered part of this category.

Paying for basic expenses

Now that you have a good idea of your basic expenses, you want to make absolutely sure they're covered by what I call guaranteed income. After all if we don't cover our basic expenses of food and shelter, the other ones really don't matter. If all we have is a finite amount of income, we'd have no choice but to spend it in this area.

So what do I mean by guaranteed income? This is any income source that will come into your bank account on a regular basis, generally without fail. Some will argue there are really no guarantees in life, but when it comes to income there are some sources that come as close to guaranteed as we can get. They're the types of income that aren't affected by the markets and that you can expect to be there as long as you are.

These sources of guaranteed income fit into two categories. The first is government pensions such as OAS and CPP in Canada or Social Security in the United States. The second is income that comes from a private source, such as a company pension plan or private annuities. And then there are "public sector pensions" if you've worked for the government during your career. Generally you want to make sure you have enough income from this category to cover your basic expenses, so you don't have to worry about the necessities of life. However, if there isn't enough income from these sources, you'll have to look to another level to help pay for the basics.

Level 2: "What if" Expenses

Once you've taken care of the basic expenses, it's time to move down the funnel to What If Expenses. Other than the need for shelter, which appears in the basic expenses section, this level addresses the essence of the issues that Maslow discusses as security needs. This is what I'd consider to be contingency, what-if, or emergency planning or anything needed for survival but that's not as important as our basic physiological needs.

As we discussed earlier in the Four Planning Cornerstones section, life happens. So our security expenses are really those expenses associated with any of these unexpected life events that may indirectly threaten our ability to pay for our basic needs. Specific expenses might include things like illness, critical illness (heart attack, cancer, stroke etc), accidents that cause bodily injury to us or physical damage to our possessions, premature death, or disability. A major concern for people in retirement is the potential costs they may incur for a long-term healthcare need.

Paying for Security Expenses

Paying for these expenses could take a few different forms. It could be a direct expense to pay for the event when it happens. Or you could systematically build up a pot of money over time that you could allocate specifically to pay for such expenses if and when they occur. The third option is to purchase insurance to share the cost of such events with a third party like an insurance company. We're talking about health, life, disability, critical illness, long-term care, as well as property and auto insurance. Property insurance could be put under basic expenses, because in some cases you can't own a home or condo without it.

By paying an insurance premium, you're paying a fraction of the ultimate cost that might be incurred if the event covered by the insurance actually occurs. You may pay premiums for a lifetime and never collect. No matter how you choose to fund your security expenses, though, a portion of your overall income should be used for this purpose.

Potential Long-Term Health Care Expenses
According to studies discussed earlier, the odds may be stacked against us later in life when it comes to potential long-term health-care needs. Long-Term Care insurance is a viable solution for this problem, yet very few people buy it. I think there are 3 main reasons why.

1. It costs too much (or at least that's the perception)

2. It's sold as an expense item, meaning it's just one more insurance premium that we have to pay.

3. Most people place themselves among those that won't ever need it

If you look at long-term care insurance as an expense item, then you'll need to find the extra cash to make the premium payment. Depending on your situation, you may have to pay for it by giving up something else. Most people choose not to do this, especially if they believe they'll never use the coverage.

At the same time as they hesitate to make premium payments for long-term health-care insurance, most people worry that the high cost of long-term healthcare, could deplete their assets. Another way to pay for this type of insurance is to re-position some of your current savings. Instead of paying the premiums from income generated by your investments and other sources, why not take a lump sum out of your savings and purchase an annuity? Then use the annuity income to pay the premiums. In this way, you use a small percentage of your overall net worth to protect it all. For an example of how this alternative funding strategy works, check out the case study in Appendix #1.

Level 3: Social Expenses

Once we've taken care of our basic needs and expenses and our security needs and expenses, we can move down to the third level of the funnel and address our social expenses. Another term to describe this category is discretionary expense. We're not required to pay for any of these things, but instead we choose to do so. For example: someone who's short on money wouldn't likely buy gifts for friends and family if he couldn't afford to put food on the table.

Once the basics are taken care of, you'll recall, Maslow's theory says we humans have a social need for belonging, love and affection. Once we have a place of shelter and we've fed and clothed ourselves, we begin to participate in social activities as a way to fill this need. Not all social activities cost money, but many do, and this is what we need to address in this section of our income plan.

Some of the basic types of social expenses include things like entertainment, hobbies, travel, gifts, memberships in community or social organizations, as well as belonging to a religious group. By no means is this a complete list. The variety of social behaviours and activities could almost be as varied as the number of people reading this book. For a detailed listing you can check out the worksheet later in this chapter or by visiting www.FearlessRetirementResources.com.

Paying for Social Expenses:
Depending on your personal income, there are two likely sources to pay for social expenses. Those who are fortunate enough to have surplus funds from their guaranteed income sources may fund some or all of these expenses from there. But many people have only enough guaranteed income to pay for the basics. These folks will need to turn to their investments to pay for discretionary social expenses.

The investments may be in the form of tax-deferred retirement savings that have been built up throughout one's working life. This may include such things as RRSPs in Canada or 401Ks in the United States. You may also have taxable investment accounts in stocks, mutual funds, segregated funds, bonds, real estate, cash value insurance policies or bank accounts. And finally, you might have Tax Free Savings Accounts (in Canada) or IRA's (in the United States). Whatever form the investments take, you have to decide which ones you'll use to provide additional income to cover social expenses.

When it comes to using our investment assets to fund our social expenses there are a couple of new issues you need to consider. First, you need to get an idea of just how much these expenses will amount to and for how long they might be applicable. Unlike our fixed/basic costs, some of these expenses may not be permanent. For instance, travel during retirement won't likely to go on forever, nor is it likely to be a flat fixed expense over time. Many people expect to spend significantly more on travel in the early years, while they're healthy, and less to none in their later years. Meeting this fluctuating expense will take a different strategy than paying for cable TV and Internet, for example, over the next 30 years.

Another point to consider here is the overall size of your investment portfolio and how much of it you need or want to allocate to these expenses. Perhaps you've decided that other needs further down the funnel are more important. Therefore they'll require a much larger portion of your overall investments, leaving you less for this area of your life.

Up to this point we've been dealing with expenses in the funnel that by and large are required or fixed expenses. Now we're starting to address expenses that could be eliminated. This is a crucial point. How you invest this portion of your money to cover these expenses will depend on how much importance you place on these social activities. If you decide that, even though they're not really required, you don't want to give them up, then you may need to create another source of guaranteed income with a portion of your investments. This will ensure they get paid for, no matter what happens. If, on the other hand, they aren't that important, then a different investment approach that doesn't create guaranteed income may be just fine for you.

Finally the old adage, It's not what you make, it's what you keep, applies to this situation. If you're trying to generate $X to pay for these expenses and you base your investment on the gross return you expect to earn, you'll most likely end up with less than you need. The decisions you make with this portion of your investments should be driven by how much you can earn on a net basis. This means the amount you get to put in your pocket to spend. To do this, you'll need to pay attention to a few key things like inflation, interest rates (if using fixed income investments), taxes, level of risk (if using variable investments), and of course fees.

The bottom line for this section of the Retirement Spending Funnel is that you need to spend some time determining what social activities are really important to you and how much they're likely to cost – realistically. Then you can look at your investment portfolio and determine how much of it you can allocate to this part of your plan. Finally, you should be able to determine the kind of investments you should use to generate the income required. Remember the goal here is to generate additional income and not dip into the capital whenever possible. How to decide all of this is covered in detail in the next chapter.

Level 4: Esteem Expenses

Esteem Expenses
(Luxury Car, Rv, Boat, Exclusive Club Membership)

As we continue to move down the funnel, we come to the level that addresses something called our Esteem Expenses. In Maslow's theory he states that, once the first three levels of needs are taken care of, people's esteem needs become increasingly important. This can include the need for things that involve our self-esteem, personal worth, social recognition, prestige, status and a sense of accomplishment. It follows, then, that anything we spend money on to achieve these things would be considered an esteem expense.

Some of the items we spend money on to enhance our sense of self-worth or to gain social recognition and status might include a recreational property in an exclusive area, an expensive boat or automobile, or a membership in an elite golf or yacht club. Some may include surgery or other medical procedures to enhance their appearance. Others may include a large donation to a charity or non-profit organization, but only if it's tied to some form of public recognition. An example is someone who donates money to a university or hospital with the expectation that a wing or building will be named after him. I'm sure you get the picture.

Paying for Esteem Expenses:

By the nature of these expenses, the amounts involved can be quite large. Because of this, it's quite often difficult to pay for them out of cash flow or income. In addition, esteem expenses are often a one-time event. For these reasons, the money will usually come from selling off an investment. This expense should fit into the overall plan without compromising other needs. Let's say, for example, you decide to buy a luxury sailboat and must sell off most of your investments to do it. You will have satisfied your esteem need and will now be part of an elite sailing club. But by the very act of selling off your investments to purchase this boat, you may no longer be able to afford your other social expenses. The point is that each of these levels is separate, yet they're also interconnected.

Unlike basic and security expenses, with social and esteem expenses, it's more about personal choice and setting priorities for yourself and your family. The choices you make will ultimately determine how much you spend and what assets you'll need to access to cover those expenses.

Level 5: Legacy Expenses

This is the final level of the Retirement Spending Funnel, and it's also the apex of Maslow's theory, which he termed Self Actualization. This is where people become self-aware and focus on fulfilling their dreams and living up to their full potential. If someone can achieve this, they can leave a legacy for future generations. This legacy may take the form of money, but sometimes it's simply about touching someone else's life in some positive way. This can be done through volunteer work, consulting, writing and educating, fundraising for a favorite cause and in many other creative and beneficial ways. So why do I call it a Legacy Expense?

No matter what kind of legacy you wish to leave, you need to allocate money for the purpose. This monetary contribution can occur either during your lifetime or upon your death. Perhaps the simplest and most common kind of legacy is to leave an inheritance to your family. Quite often, I've heard clients say they've worked hard all of their lives and managed to save some money, but they don't ever expect to spend it completely. Their purpose or potential becomes a simple gift to the next generation. They want their kids or grandkids to be just a bit better off than they were in their younger years.

Self-actualized people are often motivated by a sense of personal responsibility and ethics and feel they must contribute to the world around them. Therefore, some will become very involved in a cause they really believe in. They'll likely want to contribute time, expertise and money along the way. By becoming totally passionate about this purpose, they see it as a way to reach their potential.

No matter what course someone takes at this stage, they're fulfilling not only their potential, but perhaps their dreams, as well. All of their other expenses are taken care of, and now they can focus on solving problems and helping others. Perhaps they'll give back to society, provide someone with a helping hand, or start a family member off with some financial assistance.

Paying for Legacy Expenses

How you pay for legacy expenses depends on the person and whether you want to leave the legacy upon death or while you're still alive. If you want to give while you're alive you must have assets set aside for this purpose. You need to make sure the money you give away will not have an effect on your financial ability to fund all your other expenses. As stated previously, setting priorities is the key to ensuring that all levels of the funnel are funded.

Another factor to consider when giving away assets is the tax effect. By giving an asset that incurs capital gains, you should ensure you've accounted for the taxes. If you make the gift while you're alive, and you end up having to pay a large tax bill, you may have fewer assets to meet other expenses. On the other hand, if you give through your estate, then taxes may significantly reduce the assets available for your beneficiaries. Depending on where you live, whom you give the money to, and how you give it, there may in fact be tax breaks for your generosity. This kind of planning is far beyond the scope of this chapter, but you do need to be aware of it.

> If you and your financial advisor can better understand how to prioritize sources of income and investments relative to needs, then you'll end up with a much more dynamic, functional and sustainable financial plan.

The other popular way to leave a legacy is through the use of life insurance. Life insurance can be a very useful and cost-effective tool to provide a legacy. In many cases, for the small cost of the insurance premium you'll be able to leave a much larger legacy than you otherwise could have. For those looking to maximize the impact they can make for others, this may be the best alternative.

Summary

I hope that wasn't too much like being back in school. At its most basic level, the Retirement Spending Funnel emphasizes that we make many of our financial decisions based on human needs. If we can understand how the two are related, then perhaps we'll have a tool to help us make more informed and ultimately better financial decisions.

As far as retirement income planning is concerned, if you and your financial advisor can better understand how to prioritize sources of income and investments relative to needs, then you'll end up with a much more dynamic, functional and sustainable financial plan. This will help ensure your income and your assets are properly split to maximize your income and minimize your overall risk. In plain language, that means you'll be able to live your retirement the way you want, without worrying about your investments and whether or not you can do all the things you've dreamed about doing.

In the next chapter, I reveal the second secret to my retirement income planning system. So flip the page and let's get to it.

Chapter 9: The new math of retirement

In the last two chapters, I discussed a couple of different ways you can match your retirement income with the expenses you expect during retirement. If you've completed the income/expense worksheet introduced in the last chapter, you will have categorized your expense needs along with listing your available sources of guaranteed income. From this exercise, you may even have concluded that you're going to have an income gap. This happens when your expenses exceed your guaranteed sources of income. This shortfall or gap will have to be covered from some other source.

At first, this may have been alarming, but don't forget that this is why you saved money for your retirement throughout your working years. Like many people, though, you may wonder whether or not your retirement savings will be sufficient to cover this gap. You may even be worried about having to do without some things that are important to you or, worse yet, running out of money altogether.

In this chapter I introduce you to a new way of thinking. I focus on how to position your savings in a way that they can provide the additional guaranteed income you need, for as long as you need it, and still leave some for your estate. In other words, what's the best way to reposition your pot of gold now that you've reached the end of the rainbow, and need to start spending it? Of course, this all has to be done while taking into account the various risks we discussed in the first half of the book. Specifically, how are you going to protect yourself from inflation, sequence of return risk, market volatility, longevity risk and advisor risk?

This is a tall order, but one that's quite attainable once you know the secret. The key is to understand the difference between conventional asset allocation and something new called product allocation. I discuss these two very different approaches to investing in this chapter. Conventional asset allocation is likely quite familiar to you. Product allocation may not be. It's a new approach, based on some pretty intense mathematical theory, and is relatively unknown. Once you see the difference between these two approaches, though, you'll begin to understand why the most widely used strategy - asset allocation – simply isn't good enough by itself to provide the kind of security you'll need for your Fearless Retirement.

Asset Allocation

Most people who have accumulated funds over the years are likely familiar with the term asset allocation. But what exactly is asset allocation? Think of it as putting your money into different sections of one big pot. Each section of the pot contains a different type of investment or asset class.

Each asset class has a different purpose. In a very broad sense there are three classes of assets. They are equity (stocks), fixed income (bonds, GICs, CDs), and cash.

Equity (stocks) is used to provide growth over the long run as well as a hedge against inflation. Fixed income (bonds etc) is used to provide stability to the overall portfolio, especially in times of market turmoil, and an income when needed. Cash is used as a stabilizer for the overall portfolio and to provide an income payment.

Asset allocation models used by financial advisors have attempted to quantify the amount of equity (stocks), fixed income (bonds) and cash you should have in your overall portfolio. To do this, a combination of factors is usually considered. They include the investor's age, when he'll need access to the money and his tolerance for risk (how conservative or aggressive he is as an investor). A very conservative investor, for example, may have little if any equity (stocks) in his portfolio because he considers it too risky, whereas an aggressive investor willing to take on more risk will likely have very little fixed income and significant amounts of equity.

It has long been held that diversification and proper asset allocation have been critical to successfully accumulating wealth. In fact, some studies have indicated that up to 90% of the success or return of any given portfolio is attributable to its asset allocation. I would agree that this is true when you're accumulating assets. However, when you enter the spending phase, asset allocation alone isn't enough.

The concept of asset allocation also comes from a time when life expectancies were much shorter and longevity risk wasn't an issue. Because of this, portfolios of days gone by didn't have to create an income stream that lasted as long as it does today. In the old days, the income stream had a better chance of lasting until it was needed for estate purposes.

Also, when it came to retirement planning in the past, the asset allocation model would dictate a progression towards a more conservative mix of assets as you approached your retirement date. In fact, an old rule of thumb in the industry states you should hold an amount of fixed income equal to your age. For example, if you're 65, you should have 65% of your portfolio in fixed income. If you're 75, then you should have 75% in bonds, and so on. Personally, I've never liked rules of thumb or found them very useful.

The overall theory is that, as you get closer to the point where you'll need the money for income, your portfolio should reflect this by having less equity. This is supposed to reduce overall risk and provide an income stream from the fixed income portion of the portfolio. One of the challenges with this is that it must be monitored regularly and changed periodically by the advisor or client. This doesn't always happen on a regular or timely basis, which is where this strategy can fall down.

A sudden market correction can have a devastating effect on the size of your portfolio, depending on how much of your portfolio is invested in equity (stocks). When such corrections do come, like the seven major ones we've had in Canada since 1969, you could lose as much as one-third of your portfolio.

Fixed income investments also go through down cycles, albeit to a lesser degree. Interest rates fluctuate up and down and, depending on the type of fixed income in your portfolio, you can end up with negative returns in that portion as well. Historically, fixed income cycles do not move in concert with equity cycles, but that doesn't necessarily mean they can't or won't. It happened in the 2008 market meltdown. Investors who had what was believed to be well-balanced asset allocation strategies saw significant declines in their assets, on both the equity and fixed income components.

> For the person who may spend 30 years in retirement, and especially for those in the retirement risk zone, asset allocation is only part of a bigger overall solution to providing a lifetime income.

When you're in the accumulation phase and you have time on your side, you can recover from such corrections with patience, guidance and a commitment to staying invested. (See table 7 for total return recovery times) But if you're in the retirement risk zone and are relying on your investment assets to provide some income, this is a whole different story.

Figure 4: Total Return Recovery

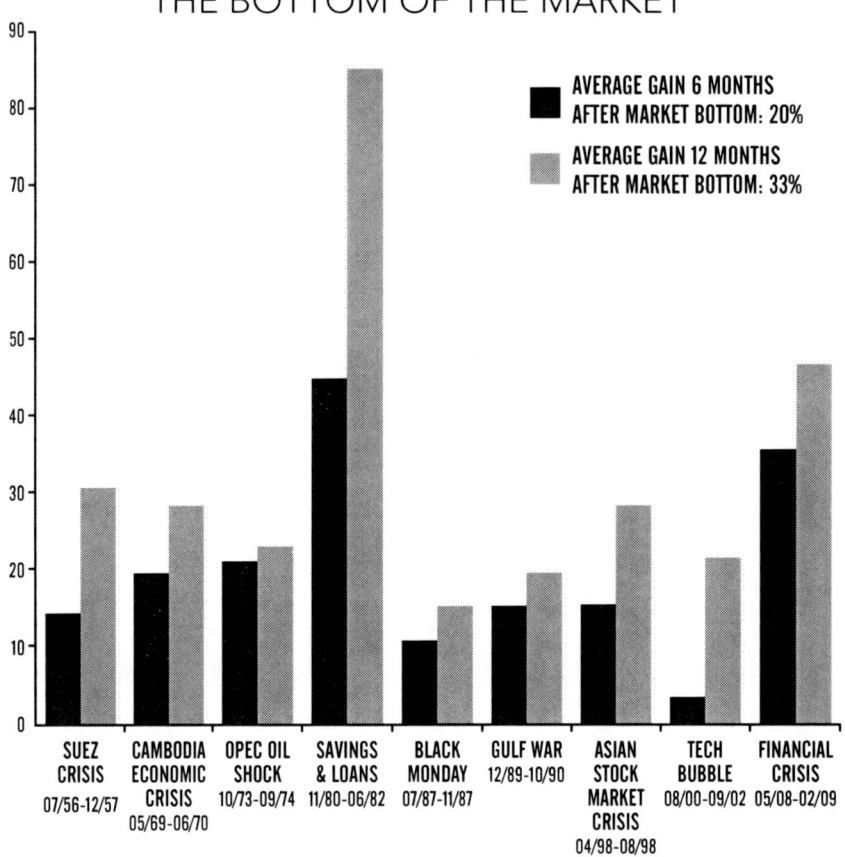

S&P/TXT TOTAL RETURN RECOVERY FROM THE BOTTOM OF THE MARKET

■ AVERAGE GAIN 6 MONTHS AFTER MARKET BOTTOM: 20%
▨ AVERAGE GAIN 12 MONTHS AFTER MARKET BOTTOM: 33%

Event	6 Months	12 Months
SUEZ CRISIS 07/56-12/57	14	30
CAMBODIA ECONOMIC CRISIS 05/69-06/70	19	28
OPEC OIL SHOCK 10/73-09/74	21	23
SAVINGS & LOANS 11/80-06/82	45	85
BLACK MONDAY 07/87-11/87	10	15
GULF WAR 12/89-10/90	15	19
ASIAN STOCK MARKET CRISIS 04/98-08/98	15	28
TECH BUBBLE 08/00-09/02	3	21
FINANCIAL CRISIS 05/08-02/09	35	46

Source: Industrial Alliance Investment Management Inc., used with permission

To address this issue in a more systematic way, some mutual fund companies have introduced lifecycle funds or target date funds. This particular category of mutual fund is designed to automatically shift the asset allocation as you move through different stages or cycles of life, based on your age or a specific amount of time. By the time retirement comes around, the portfolio may be mostly in fixed income (bonds and cash). At the end of the day, you may indeed be protected from market volatility, but the assets may not last a lifetime because of the lower returns on the fixed income investments and the effects of inflation and taxation. Nor are these lifecycle funds completely immune to major market meltdowns, although the effects may be much less as you approach retirement.

The asset allocation approach has made good sense for past generations. It was a way to help protect the nest egg as you accumulated assets and to a lesser degree as you approached retirement. But for the person who may spend 30 years in retirement, and especially for those in the retirement risk zone, asset allocation is only part of a bigger overall solution to providing a lifetime income.

Product Allocation

If asset allocation isn't the complete answer, what can you do to ensure your retirement assets last longer than you do? For the answer to this question we're going to take a field trip (figuratively speaking) to the Schulich School of Business at York University, Toronto. This is where we find Dr. Moshe Milevsky, a professor who's involved with the Quantitative Wealth Management Analytics Group (QWeMA). They've developed a retirement income analysis tool based on something they call **Product Allocation for Retirement Income (PrARI®) algorithmic methods.**

Ouch, just saying that hurts. Stay with me, though. I promised that I wouldn't get too technical, and I'll keep my promise.

To learn the second secret to creating a lifelong income you can't outlive, you need to understand the basics of this groundbreaking research and how it's different than asset allocation. This is the last piece of the puzzle, that, when added to the information in the preceding chapters, will allow you to build a rock-solid retirement income plan. So take a deep breath, get a beverage and a snack if you have to, and then we're off to learn a new way to position your pot of gold.

According to Dr. Milevsky, "Everything changes when people start to spend their savings in retirement. Their success or failure after they retire will hinge more on the type of investment products they own - product allocation – including protection and guarantees, rather than just what types of assets they own. And with the ongoing demise of Defined Benefit Pensions a new set of risks such as longevity, inflation and sequence-of-returns risk threaten chances of financial retirement success."

Having read a number of the research papers put out by QWeMA, and spending some time with Dr. Milevsky and his team, I think their research attempts to answer two simple questions: Of all the products available to retirees today, and there are a lot of them, which ones should they own? And in what proportions should they own them to reduce the chances of running out of money in retirement?

Let's take a closer look at product allocation.

If you recall when we discussed asset allocation we talked about having one pot for your money that was divided into several sections. If that pot had a tap on the bottom, you could turn it on to provide yourself with an income once you required it. Your income however is dependent on how well those three types of assets work together.

Product allocation, by contrast, uses several individual pots rather than one divided into several sections. Each product-allocation pot contains one of three specific types of income-generating products. When the time comes to draw an income, you may turn on multiple taps instead of one. And depending on the product, some income will be guaranteed and some will not be guaranteed.

The three broadly defined product types are:

Managed Money with a systematic withdrawal plan (SWP)- A managed money account can be found in many forms. The most common types are: a mutual fund, a segregated fund, a pooled investment, a stock and bond portfolio, a portfolio of GIC's or CD's, or a separately managed account (SMA). Such accounts generally have fees associated with their management.

A SWP is defined as a service whereby a portion of the managed investment account is systematically sold in order to produce a regular income. This is most commonly associated with mutual funds, but could be used in any managed account. Depending on the type of managed account, a traditional asset allocation strategy could be used within this product category.

Traditional Life Annuity – Also known as Single Premium Immediate Annuity (SPIA). Annuities are purchased from an insurance company, by making a lump sum "premium deposit" to the insurance company. In exchange for your money the insurance company will provide you with a set amount of guaranteed lifetime income. When purchasing a SPIA, you give up all future access to your capital (money) in exchange for the income stream it provides.

How much income one receives for their "premium deposit" is based on a formula that uses a number of factors, including but not limited to the following: current interest rates, age and sex of the depositor (annuitant), life expectancy of the annuitant, and guarantee period on the annuity if any.

Annuities can be purchased individually or jointly with a spouse. They can be purchased with tax deferred retirement money or non-registered taxable money. Another feature of many annuities is a guarantee period. This is where the insurance company will guarantee to make payments for a minimum time period even if the person buying the annuity dies before that time period is up. This helps to insure that the annuitant or his estate receive a minimum amount of their capital back over time.

Guaranteed Living Income Benefit (GLIB) – in the Canadian market place this is commonly known as a Guaranteed Minimum Withdrawal Benefit (GMWB). In simple terms a GLIB could be best described as a combination of a managed money account with an income stream like in an annuity. When you purchase a GLIB, sold only through life insurance companies, your money in managed in a segregated fund where you retain full access and control of it. There are significant fees attached to this managed money, with additional fees charged to guarantee the income.

In addition to the underlying investment in the segregated fund, there is an included feature or sometimes an add-on rider, which provides for a guaranteed income. This income is guaranteed provided specific contract conditions are met, and will pay out no matter how the underlying investment performs.

There are as many different additional features as there are companies that offer these products. The majority of these products have certain features that have the potential to increase the income over time if the market rises. A traditional asset allocation strategy, leaning to significant fixed income investments is generally used within this product category.

Similar to asset allocation, the overall idea with product allocation is to reduce risk, but with the added focus of providing a sustainable income for life. A combination of the three product types is used, with each product being chosen based on its ability to deal with a specific risk. For instance, managed money with a SWP is better at overcoming inflation compared to an Annuity or a GLIB. A Life Annuity is the best of the three at eliminating longevity risk. And by comparison, the Guaranteed Living Income Benefit (GLIB) is the best at addressing sequence of return risks. According to the QWeMA model, this is referred to as Risk Management Attributes.

Table 7: Product Allocation Risk Management Attributes

	Inflation	Sequence of Returns	Longevity
Life Annuity **(SPIA)**	Poor	Fair	Good
Managed Money with a **(SWP)**	Good	Poor	Poor
Guaranteed Living Benefit **(GLIB)**	Fair	Good	Fair

* Used with Permission   Source: THE QWEMA GROUP, 2009

As you can see from Table 7, no single product is best at dealing with all the major risks. Because of this, when developing a product allocation strategy, you need a combination of all three. But which of these products should you own? And how much of each should you have? The quick answer is - that depends. Generally you may need some of each.

Product allocation is based on each individual's personal situation and takes into account a number of factors. The rest of this chapter will address the other factors to consider when setting up a product allocation strategy.

Other Major Considerations of Product Allocation

According to the model developed by Professor Milevsky and his associates, there are a number of other factors to consider besides risk management when you set up a product allocation strategy. These factors are called goal-achievement attributes. The last factor is fees and expenses associated with the specific products.

Goal-Achievement Attributes:

There are three goal-achievement attributes you should consider when setting up a product allocation strategy. They are:

1. Liquidity (having access to your capital)
2. Behavioural Weaknesses (acting on emotions at the wrong time)
3. Estate Wishes (what you want to leave to your beneficiaries)

Liquidity (Access)

If you need access to lump sums of your capital over time, then liquidity will be an important factor when choosing which products to include in your product allocation. Some of the common things that may require lump sums include: the outright purchase of a vehicle for yourself or an adult child/grandchild, providing a down payment on a home for a child/grandchild, paying for a wedding for a child/grandchild or a major dream vacation. In fact, it could be anything that can't easily be paid for out of your regular income stream.

Behavioral Weaknesses (Emotions)

This refers to the likelihood of people to do the wrong thing at the wrong time when they let emotions drive their decisions. (Remember the Dalbar study from chapter 2) A prime example is when we are going through a major market correction. As much as most people know they should leave their money invested, fear often takes over and people cash out at the bottom of the market. Greed too is another emotion that leads people to invest at the top of the market, just before it's ready to go down. If you tend to be a person who reacts in this manner, you may want to emphasize products that can protect you at times like this. This would mean leaning more towards annuities and GLIBs rather than managed money with SWP.

Estate Wishes (Your Legacy)

If you wish to leave an estate for your family or charity, you'll likely tend towards products that leave you in control of your capital. You'll want access to it to leave a legacy. This could mean using less of a traditional life annuity, because such a product generally hands over control of your asset to the insurance company in exchange for a lifetime income for you.

Table 8: Product Allocation Goal-Achievement & Fee Attributes

	Liquidity	Behavioral	Estate	Fees & Expenses
Life Annuity (SPIA)	Poor	Good	Poor	Good
Managed Money with a (SWP)	Good	Poor	Good	Fair
Guaranteed Living Benefit (GLIB)	Poor	Fair	Fair	Poor

* Used with permission   Source: THE QWEMA GROUP, 2009

As you can see from Table 8, no single product best addresses all of the goal-achievement attributes. More so than with the Risk Management Attributes, this part of the strategy will be driven by what's truly important to you with respect to money – your goals and aspirations. Having a good understanding of the Retirement Spending Funnel outlined in Chapter 8 will be very helpful when considering your product allocation and the goal achievement attributes. Also, understanding how you might behave in certain situations like a major market meltdown will provide you with some guidance in your product selection.

Fees and Expenses:

With respect to fees and expenses for the three product categories, you can see that there is also considerable difference in how they're scored. The Life Annuity has the best score for fees – meaning the fees are the lowest – whereas the GLIB has the worst score because of the relatively high fees associated with this type of product. When it comes to managed money with a SWP fees can vary widely depending on the underlying investment and who is managing it for you.

Summary

When trying to decide which combination of products is best for your individual situation, it all boils down to making compromises based on your unique situation. Each product varies in how well it can deal with risk and in its ability to achieve the specific goals that may be important to you. Also, cost must be considered.

When selecting one product over another, its specific benefit will come at the expense of the benefit of the other products. For example, by using a life annuity you get lifetime income without market worries, but you may lose the benefit of leaving a legacy. By selecting only a managed money product with a SWP, you may achieve your legacy goal of retaining control of your assets, but you'll be subject to market fluctuation and sequence of return risk with respect to your income payments from that investment. Putting all your money into a GLIB plan will cost you significantly more in fees, with potentially less liquidity than a SWP, but you'll have dealt with sequence of return risk.

The big question is how do you determine the best combination of products in a product allocation strategy? Put another way, how do you match your investments to your specific income needs, based on your expenses and other factors outlined in the product allocation theory?

QWeMA have developed a set of tools based on their complex mathematical formulas to help determine what they call the "retirement sustainability quotient – RSQ". In simple terms the RSQ is a way to measure the probability that a certain combination of products will be able to sustain your desired retirement income. A zero RSQ implies that there is no chance that the chosen products can sustain your income for life. An RSQ of 100 would imply that the generated income could be guaranteed for life. To find out more about this approach to product allocation, check out a book by Moshe A. Milevsky and Alexandra C. Macqueen called *Pensionize Your Next Egg*.

For the purposes of this book I won't be using QWeMA's tools. Instead I'll show you how I combine the basic concept of product allocation with my Retirement Spending Funnel to create a retirement income plan. I call this The Fearless Retirement Blueprint and it's covered in Chapter 13. I've left it for the end of the book because it's a hands on chapter that requires some work on your part. It brings together a few simple worksheets with the Retirement Spending Funnel and a tool called the Funding Matrix.

Before you get to it and roll up your sleeves I need to address one more important issue. Chapters 10, 11 and 12 discuss how to find and select the right kind of advisor to assist you with your planning.

A note about QWeMA Group

Dr. Milevsky is the Chairman and CEO of QWeMA Group, founded in 2005 with two colleagues at York University, Professor Huaxiong Huang and Professor Thomas Salisbury, to help commercialize the optimization algorithms they developed.

While they did not invent Product Allocation, their objective was to implement it in a way that would be intuitive and applicable. The idea of allocating some retirement wealth to annuities (fixed, variable and GLWBs) was "discovered" in the 1960's by Professor Menachem Yaari (Yale University economist at the time). The day-to-day activity of the QWeMA Group is now managed by COO Faisal Habib.

Chapter 10: Financial Advisor Checklist

OK. You've made it through the tough part. Now you understand what you'll need to provide a lifetime income that you can't outlive. One problem may still remain. Either you don't have a financial advisor to help you with the plan, or you're not sure that the advisor you do have is right for the job. Not any advisor will do. Your life savings and future income are at stake. There's no room for major mistakes. You need a qualified and professional advisor, specializing in retirement income planning for this stage of your life.

No one wants to be a victim of the next Bernie Madoff. Nor does anyone want to wake up one day and discover that they owe thousands of dollars in taxes, because the tax shelter they purchased several years ago really was too good to be true. Keeping in mind the financial advisor risks that we discussed in chapter 4, you might wonder whether it's possible to protect yourself from unqualified, unethical or unlicensed advisors. The short answer is yes you can. But it takes a bit of research and applied knowledge. You can't eliminate the risk completely, since we're dealing with human nature. But you can come close.

> You can't eliminate the risk completely, since we're dealing with human nature. But you can come close.

Most people don't know what to look for in an advisor or how to check out the candidates. In this chapter you'll find the key factors to consider when you conduct your own reference checks on a potential new advisor. First we need to discuss how to get the names of a few potential candidates.

Referrals

To find a new advisor, most people ask friends, family or co-workers for a referral. This seems to be the best and safest way to find a candidate, right? After all, if Uncle Barney trusts his guy or gal with all his money, then the advisor must be OK.

In the past I'd have said this was probably true. But things have changed dramatically in today's complex financial world. Now I'd say this should be just the starting point. The infamous Bernie Madoff, who ran the biggest investment scam of all time, reportedly got most of his clients by referral only. In his clients' minds, he was a trusted advisor, and they had no reservations about introducing him to others.

If you studied the personality traits of some of the world's greatest scammers and con-artists, you'd find similarities among them. They'd be charismatic, well-spoken, good storytellers, friendly, empathetic and seemingly quite trustworthy. If you were already dealing with them, you'd share them with your friends. And this is what they hope for.

Your Own Research

What if a family member or friend doesn't provide a referral to a supposedly trusted advisor? You'll have to do some searching on your own. In days gone by you might have simply looked in the Yellow Pages for the best ad and made some calls. Today you'd likely search through the Internet to find some local candidates. Heck, there are even industry-sponsored web sites that list advisors in your city. Once you find them, you can check out their websites and marketing material to see what they have to offer, and then call a few and interview them.

A Matter of Trust

As the old saying goes, if it looks like a duck, walks like a duck and quacks like a duck, it must be a duck. If someone says he's a financial advisor and he gains your trust, there's a pretty good chance that you'll hire him, especially if the referral came from a close friend or family member. There's still a problem, though. The business of money management depends on trust, not only in the advisors, but in the companies they represent.

This is where the picture becomes blurred. There's a huge difference between someone who seems trustworthy and calls herself a financial advisor and a professional financial advisor whom you can really trust. That statement is worth repeating. There's a huge difference between someone who seems trustworthy and calls herself a financial advisor and a professional financial advisor whom you can really trust. The question is – how can you tell the difference?

The good old days of sizing someone up and hiring someone based on how you feel about them may be gone forever. This is true whether you've been given a referral or you found the advisor on your own. Unless you check out and verify a few simple yet very important things about the person, blind trust can't ensure the protection of your money or your financial future.

The financial services industry itself also fails to protect you, and for one simple reason. It's focused on profits and isn't really too concerned about the few bad apples in its midst. Sure, the industry has compliance rules in place, but at the end of the day the almighty dollar is really what matters. Unfortunately, the regulatory bodies, try as they might, can't always protect you either.

A Chinese proverb says, "You cannot serve two masters at the same time." I believe this applies to the regulatory bodies in Canada. For the most part, they're self regulatory, which means they're funded by the industry they oversee, and not by a third party like the government. So how can they effectively serve you, the consumer, and the companies that pay their salaries at the same time? They can't!

Major fraud cases involving billion-dollar swindles get lots of media attention, while many other cases go unnoticed by the masses. Yet these smaller cases affect thousands of clients. You don't have to look very hard to find a number of cases that clearly illustrate how the industry and its regulators have failed to protect the consumer.

I came across one such case a few years ago. Several advisors at a registered firm had their securities licenses permanently revoked. These individuals were no longer licensed to sell any legitimate securities such as stocks, bonds or mutual funds. Yet they remained in business selling what they called "investments" and "tax shelters". Neither of which were regulated. Allegedly, one of the advisors even retained an insurance license, which allowed them to sell all kinds of insurance products. This included segregated funds.

The tax shelter was eventually investigated by the federal government's tax department. If they rule against this "tax shelter" then clients who bought it could have their

> There's a huge difference between someone who seems trustworthy and calls herself a financial advisor and a professional financial advisor whom you can really trust.

taxes reassessed and have to pay hefty penalties. To make matters worse, they may also lose their original investment, with no recourse. Once again, the system has let the consumer down. These individuals were banned from holding a securities license, they were under active investigation by the federal tax department, yet they were still able to sell an unregulated tax shelter investment. Talk about pretzel logic!

The bottom line is that the regulators under the current fragmented structure in Canada are limited in their powers to protect the public. Major cases get media attention. But for every one of those, how many others never even register on the radar? Without a coordinated national securities regulator with legal powers to prosecute offenders, and enforce financial judgments, things won't get better for the thousands of victims in this country. Until that happens, the best way you'll get protection is to take matters into your own hands and learn how to protect yourself. So let's get to it and learn some basic steps.

What to Check

Years ago, formal home inspections were a rarity. Sure, Uncle Buck or your friend Bill the Builder may have dropped by to check it out, but that was about it. Today, almost nobody buys a home without a home inspection. I know some enterprising real estate agents who provide sellers with a full home inspection, at their cost, of the homes they list. Why the radical shift to home inspections?

It's simple really. If you're going to spend $150,000, $300,000 or $1,000,000 on a property, you want to ensure that it's worth it. You want to make sure the foundation's solid, there are no leaks in the roof, the furnace is up to par, and the plumbing and wiring all work and are up to code. After all, this is a huge investment, right? It's an investment!

So what the heck does a home inspection have to do with hiring a financial advisor?

Everything.

Let me ask you a question. Why would you spend money to inspect an investment in a home and not spend money to inspect the person handling your other investments?

In my opinion, you must check out potential financial advisors before you buy into them and their services. It's nothing personal, it's just good business. If you're going to hand over $100,000 or $500,000 of your money, you want to know it will be safe.

You're probably thinking that financial advisors aren't like houses. There are no mechanical systems to check out, no foundation to survey, and no shingles to inspect. Until mid-2009, I would have thought the same thing. But at that time, the media were full of stories of swindlers, scammers and thieves that had wreaked economic ruin on unsuspecting and trustworthy consumers. This was nothing new, but the frequency and severity of the stories was, and it started to concern me. I knew there were some simple things people could do to check out an advisor. So why weren't people doing them?

My first reaction to most scandals is usually: how gullible can people be? But then I realize – people aren't gullible. People are honest, hardworking and trusting individuals who simply don't know what they don't know.

Then one day, I had an "a-ha" moment. It was triggered by a strange email from one of my best clients. We'd been working together for about six years and had what I thought was a very good working relationship. However, in light of the most recent investment scandal, he suddenly wanted to know all kinds of things about my business. In his email he asked very pointed questions about my qualifications, my licensing, my ongoing education, and the compliance systems in place at my firm to protect his money.

We met to discuss the answers. He explained that he wasn't really concerned with me, but he'd been doing some reading and felt it was the prudent thing to do, given the nature of the work I was doing for him. Fair enough, I said. I went through every question, one by one, in considerable detail, and gave him all the evidence and re-assurance he wanted.

For me, this was a major wake-up call! If one of my best, most informed clients was asking these kinds of questions, were any of my other clients concerned too? And if they were, would they take the time to do the research he'd done just to figure out the right questions to ask? What about all the other consumers out there?

In my "a-ha" moment it occurred to me that there are certain fundamental things every advisor must have present in his or her business that makes them not only legitimate but professional. These things form the foundation of a professional financial advisory business. They're also associated with certain codes or rules that must be followed. Every client who's going to deal with a financial advisor should know about them up front before doing business. Unfortunately, most of them have no idea about this stuff.

> **Why would you spend money to inspect an investment in a home and not spend money to inspect the person handling your other investments?**

I had all of these fundamentals covered in my business, but obviously I hadn't communicated it effectively to my clients. Good for my client, I thought, for doing this work and bringing these concerns to me.

This encounter prompted me to come up with the idea of the **Financial Advisor Checklist.** This checklist covers the 13 most critical things you should check about any advisor before you hire him.

Now let's get down to the basics of protecting yourself and your money.

The Financial Advisor Checklist

Here are 13 of the most basic things you should check before you deal with any financial advisor. You can begin simply by obtaining the prospective advisor's business card or visiting his website. Much of the information needed is publicly available and can be obtained with relative ease. If victims of a recent scam in Montreal had simply done the first thing on this list, they could have avoided completely the financial ruin they now face. In fact, many cases of theft and fraud involving so-called financial advisors were perpetrated by scammers who were not even licensed to sell investments anywhere.

1. Is the person licensed to sell investments in your province or state?

2. Does he have an investment dealer, and who is it?

3. Is he in good standing with that firm? Are there any disciplinary actions on file? Is he working under any "strict supervision orders"?

4. What regulatory body is the firm governed by – MFDA, IIROC, SEC other?

5. Is he and his firm in good standing with the regulatory body – that is, are there any disciplinary actions, cease-trade orders, suspensions, or bans on file against the advisor or the firm?

6. If he's not licensed to sell investments, is he licensed to sell insurance products including annuities and variable annuities in your province or state?

7. Who is his insurance dealer/broker/managing general agency?

8. What regulatory body, if any, is his insurance dealer governed by?

9. Is he and his firm in good standing with that Insurance regulatory body – that is are there any disciplinary actions on file?

10. Is the person a licensed Financial Planner? Does he hold a CFP designation?

11. Is he a member in good standing of the governing bodies for the designations he holds?

12. Has he ever declared personal or corporate bankruptcy?

13. Are the any media stories about this advisor – good or bad?

13 questions: How to get answers

Arguably the biggest stumbling block for most people is how to go about checking out these 13 questions. It's great to know what to check out, but this is helpful only if you know where to turn to do the checking.

The prospective advisor's business card is a good place to start. In most jurisdictions, there are mandatory requirements to present certain information on the business card. Of course there are the basics like name, address and phone number. But beyond this the card must carry the dealer name and may disclose that the firm is a member of a certain regulatory body. If you don't have the business card, at the very least you'll need to obtain the name of the advisor, his business address his dealer's name and whether or not he has any professional designations – CFP, CLU, CA, CSA etc.

Step 1: Is the advisor licensed by a securities commission?

To find out if a person is licensed to sell securities, you need to contact your provincial securities commission. (In the U.S., contact the state or federal securities commission.) All of the securities commissions have websites where you can do this without speaking to anyone. (I provide some examples later.) In Canada, however, there's no national regulator or securities commission. Each province has its own. As a result, the level of detail and tools available vary widely on these sites from province to province. Some, like the B.C. Securities Commission, have a very user-friendly and useful site.

The point is, depending on where you live in Canada, the provincial commission's web-based search tools can be a challenge. You'll need time and patience or you may get misleading results. There is an alternative. As mentioned in Chapter 5 the Canadian Securities Administrators (CSA) is an informal body with representation from all the securities commissions in Canada. The CSA has developed a national registration database (NRD) of all registered advisors in Canada. One of the key tools is a search tool on the CSA's website, at **www.securities-administrators.ca,** which enables investors to see if an advisor is registered. Unfortunately this search tool does not include advisors from Ontario, and omits certain "conditions" for those advisors registered in Quebec. If you live in either of these provinces you'll have to go to your provincial securities commission.

The CSA search tool is a good place to start, but if you want more detailed information you may have to go to your province's securities commission site.
Alternatively, you can contact your regional securities commission by telephone and request the information. If you do, you'll need the same basic information – the advisor's name, business address and firm.

Figure 4: Contact information

In Canada: The Canadian Securities Administrators: www.securities-administrators.ca
In the U.S. The Securities and Exchange Commission (SEC): www.sec.gov

For a list of Securities Commissions and their contact information visit:
www.FearlessRetirementResources.com

Once you determine the person is, in fact, licensed, you may want to check out a couple of other things at the securities commission. Again the amount of information available depends on the particular commission. You may want to determine how long the person has been licensed and how many dealer firms he's worked for over the years. Moving from firm to firm may indicate some internal disciplinary problems. Perhaps the advisor is churning his book, getting paid over and over again on the same investments by moving them from company to company. On the other hand, he may have a legitimate reason for moving, so you'll need to investigate this further.

You may also see if the person's license has been suspended over the years or if the commission has placed an order upon him. You can see if his name appears on a Cease Trade List, or if he's on a list of Disciplined Persons. These lists can be found at the website of your provincial securities regulator or the Canadian Securities Administrators.

In any case, if he's not currently licensed, you should determine when he was last licensed to sell securities and the reason why he's no longer licensed. Again, you'll need to dig a little deeper. If you find the advisor's not currently licensed, he may have a legitimate reason.

For instance, in certain states of the U.S., some advisors do not have to be registered with the SEC, but register instead with a state regulator. And in Canada there is something known as the Northwestern Exemption Orders. This applies only to specific western provinces and northern territories. Under this exemption, individuals and firms are exempt from the dealer registration requirements of National Instrument 31-103. Essentially this allows anyone in these specific regions to sell high-risk exempt market products to the investing public without being registered and with no oversight.

Also in Canada, an advisor may have given up his securities license to sell only segregated funds under an insurance license.

Finally, you should identify the self-regulatory organization (SRO) with whom the person's dealer may be registered. Canadian dealers who belong to an SRO will be members of either the Mutual Fund Dealers Association (MFDA) or the Investment Industry Regulatory Organization of Canada (IIROC). (This information will be required to complete step #2)

A search in action

I did a random search on the B.C. Securities site and found an advisor who has been licensed since 2001. On further investigation, I found that he has worked with two different dealers in that time. Not a big deal. He changed because his original dealer had been purchased by another. He has never had his license suspended, but he has had three supervision orders placed on his license. In 2006, he was given an order to work under strict supervision, which he agreed to. In 2008 he was given another order to be closely supervised. And later in 2008, when he changed dealers, a new order for close supervision was issued, continuing the previous one.

So what does this tell us? It tells us that he is currently licensed by a legitimate authority called the B.C. Securities Commission. He has never had his license suspended, but he has received three supervision orders, which merit further investigation. In fact, some people might take this advisor off their list of candidates. They may want someone who has been in the business longer, or they would rather deal with someone who hasn't been placed under strict supervision.

In this first step, you may discover that an advisor has never been licensed. If he has been licensed, you may find the license has been suspended or terminated. This should raise a big red flag. You will likely exclude this person from your list of possible advisors. But if an advisor's license is perfectly clean, with no suspensions or supervisory orders, or if there are some minor issues, you may move on to the next step and contact the advisor's regulatory organization.

Step 2: Contact the regulatory organization that oversees the advisors dealer

Once an advisor in Canada gets his license from a securities commission, he must find an investment dealer. The type of securities registration determines the type of dealer and the kinds of products he can sell. For instance, someone licensed to only sell mutual funds will likely use an MFDA dealer. Someone licensed to sell stocks, bonds, ETF's, Limited Partnerships (LP's) as well as mutual funds will likely work with an IIROC-registered dealer. It's important to note that IIROC registers (licenses) their own advisors, whereas the MFDA does not. Advisors with an MFDA firm are licensed through their provincial securities commission and then registered with the CSA. Confused? This is one more reason why Canada needs a single national securities regulator.

Unfortunately for the consumer in Canada, not all investment dealers are required to belong to an SRO. The first thing to check after you've confirmed the advisor is registered with the securities commission is whether or not his dealer is a member of an SRO. If the dealer isn't an SRO member, you may want to find out why or eliminate them from your list of choices.

For dealers that are members of an SRO, the SRO's job is to directly oversee both the dealer firm and by extension the advisor's activity. If your prospective new advisor works for one of these dealers, you should check that both the advisor and his dealer firm are in good standing with the SRO. Are there any past disciplinary actions, orders, suspensions, or bans on file against either the advisor or the dealer? Keep in mind that current complaints that have not escalated to the hearing level will not show up on a search at these SROs.

Before you begin, you need to know whether the dealer firm falls under the MFDA or IIROC. You should have determined this in step one. If in doubt, call the advisor's dealer firm. With this information, you can go to the SRO's website or call the organization directly.

SRO's In Canada:

MFDA: Website: **www.mfda.ca** Phone: 1-888-466-6332
IIROC: website: **www.iiroc.ca** Phone: 1-866-214-7200

MFDA Search

If the advisor's dealer is a member of the MFDA, you can do a search on the MFDA website. In general what you will be looking for is a section on Enforcement. Once you locate that, you can then determine if any past or current notices of hearings have been listed for the advisor or his dealer. *Keep in mind that if an investigation has not yet led to a notice of hearing, there will be no information posted.* If you are unable to find what you're looking for on the website, you can always call the MFDA directly at the number listed above.

In mid 2010, the MFDA announced that at some future date it will provide the CSA with information on its registered advisors in an effort to give consumers a single point of access to check out the disciplinary history of an advisor. As it stands today information in the CSA disciplined persons database comes only from the provincial securities commissions and not the SRO's, so you have to look in two places to get the full picture.

IIROC Search

If the advisor and her firm are registered with IIROC, you can do the research on that organization's site. Historically, IIROC didn't make it easy to search on its website for information on disciplinary action taken against their registered firms or dealers, or get comprehensive registrant information.

This all changed in mid 2010 with the new "Advisor Report" found in the Know Your Advisor section of the IIROC website. Not only can you easily confirm that the prospective advisor is approved (licensed) to work at an IIROC –regulated firm, but you can find out what functions and roles they have been approved to perform. In addition this report provides a listing of the advisors educational background specific to any courses taken to fulfill the regulators "proficiency requirements". And lastly, you can see if there is any disciplinary history for the advisor. Keep in mind that this search tool is only applicable for current registrants. Finding information on a past registrant will require you to use the Consolidated Enforcement Actions section on the website.

FAIR Canada Research Study

If you did nothing else but check to see if the person you are considering is a registered advisor, you would at least protect yourself against the unregistered fraudsters looking to separate you from your money. But is this enough? I don't believe it is. This also seems to be the conclusion of a recent study conducted by the Canadian Foundation for

Advancement of Investors Rights (FAIR Canada). FAIR is an independent non-profit organization that represents the interests of Canadian investors in securities regulations. Its study, completed in early 2010, indicates that registration is no indication that the firm at which a particular advisor is registered is necessarily a safe one to deal with.

The FAIR Canada study looked at the biggest financial scams in Canada from 1999 to the end of 2009. Of 15 cases examined, the majority were Ponzi-type schemes. FAIR estimated the financial loss to investors to be about $2 billion. About 80% of the losses involved **registered firms**. The surprising finding was that only "9% of those losses could be traced back to firms that belonged to a self-regulatory organization (MFDA or IIROC)". It's important to remember that there are exemptions in Canada that allow certain dealers to operate without belonging to an SRO. These exempt firms accounted for the majority (91%) of the losses in this study.

> If you did nothing else but check to see if the person you are considering is a registered advisor, you would at least protect yourself against the unregistered fraudsters looking to separate you from your money.

From this study, one could conclude that dealing with a firm that's a member of an SRO may have provided a greater level of protection. However, it would seem that dealing with a registered firm still did not completely protect Canadians from being a victim of one of these 15 major scams. Also, if SROs are really doing a better job of policing their members, then why aren't ALL registered firms required to belong to an SRO? To view the full results of the FAIR Canada study, you can visit **www.faircanada.ca**.

The bottom line is that neither the provincial securities regulators nor the SROs can completely protect investors in Canada. This is why you need to take it upon yourself to do further research into any financial advisor if you're going to entrust him to manage your life savings. Let's take a look at some more things you can do.

Step 3: Contact the potential advisor's dealer firm

By this point you've determined whether or not the potential advisor is licensed by a securities commission, if he's registered with a dealer firm and if there are any disciplinary actions against him at the SRO, assuming his firm is required to be a member. Now you can contact the firm to do some additional checking. If you feel comfortable with your findings to this point, this step may not be necessary. But if you've found discrepancies in the advisor's record, such as conditions or disciplinary actions attached to his registration, you may want to investigate further. Some people will end their search and reject the advisor if they discover disciplinary actions against him. Keep in mind, though, that these can involve a minor situation that can be clarified with an explanation.

If you proceed with your search, some dealers may refuse to give you any information, using privacy as an excuse. Other dealers will provide information up to a point. This is not surprising, given that dealers have a vested interest in the fees generated by their advisors. Keep in mind that the point of this part of your research is to get secondary information to corroborate findings from your search at the SRO and securities regulators. If a dealer is unwilling to provide additional details regarding matters of public record like suspensions, supervisory actions or cease-trade orders, then this may not be a dealer or advisor you want to work with.

Some of the things you may ask about the advisor include:

1. How long has the advisor been with the firm?

2. Has he had any issues that required supervisory action?

3. Has the dealer taken any internal disciplinary action that didn't involve its regulator?

4. If there's a public record of disciplinary action or conditions placed on the advisor, can the dealer expand on the reasons or give any additional insight?

5. Does the advisor have current and up-to-date error and omission (E&O) insurance coverage?

6. Are there any referral arrangements on file with the dealer that may be considered a conflict of interest?

Some things you might want to ask about the firm include:

1. Is the dealer firm dealing with any current regulatory issues?

2. If there's a public record of disciplinary action against the firm, can the firm provide you with some insight into it?

3. What internal compliance systems does the firm have in place to keep itself and its advisors in line with all regulatory requirements?

4. How do the firm's branches supervise the advisor in question? Specifically, does the branch manager or person overseeing trades have a financial interest in the business being placed?

5. How does the firm's complaint resolution process work?

Step 4: Check to see if the advisor is licensed to sell insurance products

Having completed steps 1-3, you may have determined that the potential advisor is not licensed to sell securities in your region. This may involve one of a couple of reasons. Either he has given up or had such registration taken away or he was never licensed to sell securities in the first place.

If he gave up his securities license or had it taken away, you should find out the reason. Depending on the reason, you may take the advisor off your list.

If he wasn't licensed at all, he may still be licensed to sell insurance. That license covers investment products offered by insurance companies.

To see if an advisor's licensed to sell insurance products, contact the insurance licensing body in the province or state where you live. As with securities, there's no national insurance regulator in Canada. To make matters worse, regulators operate under different names in each province and territory. In Ontario for instance you need to contact the Financial Services Commission of Ontario. In Manitoba the agency governing insurance is the Insurance Council of Manitoba.

You'll need to identify the agency in your province or territory and contact it. You can find a list of the various agencies at www.FearlessRetirementResources.com or at the Canadian Council of Insurance Regulators www.ccir-ccrra.org which is an inter-jurisdictional association of regulators of insurance. In the United States you can check for insurance registrations at the National Association of Insurance Commissions (NAIC). Their website is www.naic.org.

Under current regulations in Canada the sale of investment products in the insurance industry resembles the wild-west. For the most part insurance agents in Canada must place their business through a Managing General Agency (MGA). MGAs, however, are not regulated by any government agency or SRO. As a result the strict compliance rules found on the securities side of the business simply don't apply to the insurance advisors' world. It is this lax regulation that has attracted many advisors to give up their securities licenses and sell only insurance based investments. There's a movement to bring segregated funds under the jurisdiction of provincial securities regulators, but the lobby against it by insurance companies and MGA's seems very strong.

Having a single national securities regulator that also covers these insurance based investments would be the ideal solution. Moving them under the MFDA or IIROC would be a good interim measure. Until that happens, the consumer needs to be aware that there are no uniform rules governing the actions of insurance advisors with respect to the standard know-your-client and investment-suitability rules that are regular practice in the mutual fund and securities world. The insurance companies don't do it. And the managing general agencies (MGA's) who have the direct relationship with insurance agents/brokers (and a financial interest) aren't required to do it either. To be fair some MGAs have chosen to operate within the structure of an MFDA or IIROC dealership. Those that are set up this way are held accountable to the regulations of their SRO.

Step 5: Professional designation search

In your search for a new retirement-income planning-focused advisor, some of the potential candidates may have one or more so-called professional designations after their names. You know what I mean – the alphabet soup following their names on their business cards. If they don't have any, you may ask yourself why. I mean, don't they take their business and their clients' needs seriously enough to learn all they can so they can give the best possible advice?

On the other hand, if they do have an alphabet soup of designations, which ones have any real credibility or value? I recently came across some interesting data in a study done for the Financial Planners Standards Council of Canada by Lynn Gordon Research. In that study, "78% of respondents who used a financial professional said this person had a financial planning designation. However, the majority (69%) of these respondents claimed they had no idea what designation was held".

Furthermore, "among all respondents, awareness of the CFP® as a financial planning designation was 10%– a recognition that was by far the highest of all designations on an unaided basis, the next (PFP) trailing at 1.5%".

Some might argue that designations are meaningless, which explains the low level of awareness among consumers. However, the same research study makes me believe otherwise. The study found that "even though many respondents were unaware if their financial professional had a professional designation and what it was, 74% indicated it was very important to have this designation"[*].

It would seem that we have a paradox when it comes to professional designations. Consumers clearly believe it's important for advisors to have designations. Yet most don't know which ones their advisors have, nor do they understand which ones mean the most to their financial well-being. If you're like the 74% of respondents in the Lynn Gordon study who believe it is very important to have a designation,

---

[*] Page 6 – Lynn Gordon Research – 2003 Study completed for FPSC

then how do you determine which ones an advisor should have?

Complicating the issue further is the fact that there are just so many designations available. According to a database published by the Financial Industry Regulatory Authority (FINRA) in the United States, there are more than 80 designations in the financial services industry. How on earth can the average consumer tell the difference between them?

By title alone, many sound very impressive. Yet if you were to dig a little deeper you'd find that just about any organization can offer a course that leads to a designation. It's no wonder there are so many to choose from. That said, very few designations have any real significance for someone seeking advice on retirement income planning.

Issues to consider

A professional designation is only one of many factors to consider. Some very qualified professional advisors don't have any designations, possibly for a very valid reason. Some of the advisors without designations have significant experience that rivals anything they could gain by acquiring a designation. They've been well trained, kept up on the latest information and act in the same way as they would if they were a fully designated advisor. They have a client-centered focus based on ethics, and they act in the best interests of their clients. By contrast, the same can't always be said for some advisors who hold several professional designations.

With this in mind, if you're trying to figure out if the designations of a prospective financial advisor are appropriate for you as a client, you should consider three key questions.

Relevance

The first question is whether or not a particular designation has *relevance* to your situation and specific financial planning needs. That is, will the knowledge and expertise that comes from having designation XYZ make a significant difference in the quality of the advice you receive?

In days gone by, you could put just about any letters you wanted after your name. In fact, I knew an advisor who had PPL on his card. So what does PPL stand for? Personal Pilots License, of course – nothing to do with financial planning. But it apparently gave him credibility. But I digress.........

Let's assume someone is looking for a comprehensive retirement income plan. She has met two prospective advisors. One has an RHU™ designation and the other has a CFP®. They both work for the same reputable firm, and they've been in the business roughly the same length of time – 20 years. Based on this information alone, which would be the best choice?

The person probably shouldn't hire the advisor who holds only the RHU™ designation. The Registered Health Underwriter designation is a specialized, yet limited, qualification in Canada that focuses on assisting clients with their living benefits needs. As such, an RHU™ advisor has specialized knowledge in selling disability, critical illness and long-term care insurance, but not necessarily in retirement income planning. The CFP® advisor would be a more appropriate choice, because of its more holistic approach to planning, including cash flow and retirement income planning.

If, on the other hand, the client was not looking for any financial planning advice at all, but instead wanted someone who was highly trained in investment portfolio construction and investment management, then she might consider someone with a Chartered Financial Analyst (CFA) designation.

Practicing the principles

Let's assume you've found someone with a relevant designation. The next question you should ask is if the advisor actually practices the principles of that particular designation? Some advisors have taken the time to get a designation, yet don't actually practice the principles that the designation represents. Even though they may be required to meet continuing education requirements and follow code of conduct, they may have no intention of using what they learned to produce written financial plans. So why do they bother to get a designation? That's a very good question.

> **Just because someone has a particular designation doesn't necessarily mean he practices the principles at the designation's core.**

Some get it because of the credibility factor – having a designation looks good on the business card. Still others are required to get one as a condition of employment. Yet these folks have no interest in putting in the time required to use it to its full potential. They may be too busy trying to fill sales quotas and win sales contests to be bothered doing all the real planning-work required when writing a financial plan. Bottom line is that just because someone has a particular designation doesn't necessarily mean he practices the principles at the designation's core.

You'll want to find out if the prospective advisor you're considering hiring does so.

In chapter 12 I'll provide you with a tool to help you determine specifically whether or not a particular advisor (designated or not) actually practices the principles of planning or is simply a transaction-based salesperson with letters after his name.

Requirements to get and keep a designation

The third key question you should ask is: What requirements must an advisor meet to get and keep a particular designation? There's an old joke about a doctor who got his degree from a Cracker Jack box. If indeed you could get a medical degree that way, would that doctor be as well trained as one who obtained hers over seven years of study and internship through a major medical university? Of course they wouldn't. Furthermore, would a sane person deal with anyone other than a university-trained doctor? That said, how is the average person supposed to know about the requirements to obtain any of the many financial designations or the difference between them?

A good place to find this information is in the database compiled by the Financial Industry Regulatory Authority

(FINRA) in the United States, which can be found at www.finra.org. Unfortunately there's no comparable Canadian database. While the following information is based on U.S. data, many of the designations are also available in Canada, through subsidiary organizations.

The FINRA database doesn't just list the names of the 80+ designations. It also provides some other useful information to help you determine not only the degree of difficulty to obtain the designation, but also its legitimacy and significance. There are also handy links to the organizations that offer the designations that you can use in your search.

Primarily this database lists:

1. Pre-requisite/experience required to apply for the course

2. Education/course requirements to obtain the designation

3. Type of exam required at the end of the course, if there is one

4. Continuing education requirements after obtaining the designation

5. Investor complaint process

6. Public disciplinary process

7. Online accessibility of a designation holder's status

8. Accreditation of the organization offering the designation

When I was going through the complete list, I began to notice significant differences between the designations with respect to the eight items listed above. Some designations have no pre-requisites or prior experience requirements at all, while others do. The level of education requirements tend to vary greatly. With respect to exams, some don't have an exam, while some are online, open book exams, and yet others are closed book proctored exams.

Once obtaining the designation, some organizations have no continuing education requirements while others have significant annual requirements. Some organizations that offer designations have no investor complaint process, while others have one, but don't publicly list any of the disciplinary actions taken against their designation holders. And finally, many of the organizations offering designations aren't accredited in any way.

The differences between the multitude of designations has reaffirmed my belief that, for someone looking for financial planning advice, including retirement income planning, the CFP® is the most valuable designation. All others are secondary.

As a profession evolves, the standards and requirements to qualify for designations will change. This applies to chartered accountants and doctors as well as financial planners, and it means not everyone will have qualified for a CFP® designation in the same way.

Back in the mid-1990s the CFP™ Board of Standards in the US and its Canadian equivalent introduced a new certification exam, which all new CFP® candidates had to write and pass. However, existing CFP® practitioners at that time were grandfathered and never had to write this exam. This doesn't mean they necessarily are less qualified. They simply qualified under different rules. The certification process will continue to change as it did again for CFP candidates in Canada in 2010. It's important to remember that all CFP® practitioners must meet the same high ethical and continuing-education standards, no matter how they got their designation.

That said, when it comes to the CFP designation, you should focus not on how someone obtained it, but rather on whether it is relevant to your needs and if so does the advisor practice the principles of that designation.

In appendix #2, I provide a mini case study that compares how the CFP® designation measures up to another designation according to information found in the FINRA database. I also provide detailed information on the new criteria for obtaining the CFP® designation in Canada pursuant to changes implemented in July 2010.

What to check and where, when it comes to designations

Now you know what to look for when checking a prospective advisor's designation. If you want to check a specific designation that your current or prospective advisor holds, you can use the resources that I've described in the previous pages. Remember though that you should also determine if the advisor is in good standing with the organization that oversees the designation. As we discussed earlier, some organizations provide this information, and others don't.

Canadian resources:

As I mentioned, there's no database of designations available in Canada. But many of the significant designations are available internationally, including the U.S. You could start your research by going to the FINRA website. Some of the information won't be exactly the same as information in Canada, but it will give you a good sense of what's involved. It is my opinion that only five designations are relevant to retirement income planning in Canada. They're listed in Table 10.

Table 9 Designations relevant to retirement income planning in Canada

Designation	Sponsoring Organization	Website
Certified Financial Planner, **CFP**	Financial Planners Standards Council of Canada (**FPSC**)	www.fpsccanada.org
Chartered Life Underwriter, **CLU** (Only if held in addition to a CPF)	The Financial Advisors Association of Canada Advocis	www.advocis.ca
Chartered Accountant, **CA** (Only if held in addition to a CFP)	Chartered Accountants of Canada	www.cica.ca
Certified Senior Advisor, **CSA** (Only if held in addition to a CFP)	Canadian Academy of Senior Advisors	www.canadacsa.com
Chartered Financial Analyst, **CFA** (Only if held in addition to a CFP)	CFA Institute	www.cfainstitute.org www.cfacanada.org

U.S. Resources

In the U.S. the best place to start this search is on the FINRA website www.finra.org. Go to the investor section of the site and look for a menu item called professional designations. It lists all the designations available in the US. Once you find the one you're looking for, you should click on the organization's link, if provided, to get more information.

Alternatively you can visit www.FearlessRetirement Resources.com to find an updated list of places to search for designation information.

A Final Word about the Profession of Financial Planning

As I've said, it's my belief that you should look for an advisor with a CFP® designation. Even though I applaud the international CFP® Boards for increasing the profile of financial planning and raising its professional standards, I don't think the industry or the regulators have kept pace. I think a CFP® designation should be mandatory for anyone who wants to enter the financial services industry, especially if he'll be advising clients on the use of their financial assets.

Many in the industry may disagree. But if financial planning is to become a profession like medicine, accounting or law, then the industry needs to act like one. Can you imagine a medical profession that allowed someone to practice without first obtaining an MD, and belonging to the medical association? Then why shouldn't a financial planner/advisor have to meet a similarly consistent and professional standard to handle your money?

In addition there should be a mandatory requirement to belong to a national professional association that oversees the activities of its members. This association, if it existed would have a strict code of ethics that must be followed, with remedies in place to disbar any member who breaks the code. Such a code could well be modeled on the CFP® Code of Ethics. And finally this association would require all members to complete substantial and meaningful continuing education each year. Unfortunately no such mandatory association exists today in Canada.

> I also believe that the financial services industry should require an apprenticeship or internship program to assist candidates who enter the industry.

I also believe that the financial services industry should require an apprenticeship or internship program to assist candidates who enter the industry. This should be run concurrently as new entrants to the industry work for three years towards their mandatory CFP® designation. New advisors would gain a wealth of real-world knowledge as apprentices to experienced planners, something they can't get by taking a course. Experience is a funny thing. You can't get it until you've had it. Once again we could learn something from the medical profession.

The consumer, meanwhile, would have access to better advice from any new advisor in the industry because of his relationship with an experienced mentor. More experienced advisors could team up with a junior advisor who could potentially take over their business when they retire. Many existing advisors will retire in large numbers over the coming decade, and their clients will face serious challenges unless enough qualified new advisors/planners take over their accounts. An apprentice program would act as a built-in succession plan to address both the clients' and the advisors' need for a smooth transition.

Step 6: Check for Bankruptcy

When I suggest to colleagues in the industry that clients should check to see if an advisor has declared bankruptcy, they usually ask me if I'm kidding. But I'm not kidding. I know that bad things can happen to good people, including good advisors, and there may in fact be a legitimate reason why someone declares bankruptcy. Under the right circumstances, beginning with full disclosure by the advisor, a client might even overlook such an event. But those circumstances don't often arise.

So why do you need this information about your financial advisor? There are two main reasons. First, anyone who holds himself out as a financial planner, advisor or counselor and who provides financial advice has no right to give such advice if she can't manage her own financial affairs. Some would argue that an advisor's personal life has nothing to do with her business life. But financial advisors help people to make decisions about money, and their own ability to handle money should be held to a much higher standard and level of scrutiny.

Second, bankruptcy for a financial advisor raises a major conflict of interest. Imagine working with an advisor who has just declared bankruptcy and is now climbing back to solvency. She hasn't disclosed this fact to you, and none of the regulators requires her to do it. This advisor, who handles all your investments, recommends a specific investment and, based on the information provided, you agree to it. Isn't it possible that the person might make recommendations in their best interest rather than yours? After all, she's trying to get her financial life back. She could probably make a logical and persuasive case for one investment over another, and you may well agree. But she's certainly not entirely disinterested in your decision or acting entirely on your behalf.

An advisor could make a number of recommendations that would benefit her more than the client, ranging from investments that pay higher commissions, regardless of their appropriateness, to charging new fees that she has never charged before. She may suggest products on a Deferred Sales Charge (DSC) basis, when in fact a client should choose a Front End Load or No-Load fund. Even though the client makes the wrong choice, the advisor gets a big commission up front from the DSC fund and locks in the investment for a number of years.

Or she might recommend rebalancing your portfolio. This isn't out of the ordinary, unless she does it in a way that generates more fees on the same money. This is called churning. It happens when a client, on the advice of his financial advisor, sells an existing investment that may or may not trigger DSC fees, and then reinvests the proceeds in a new fund that pays a commission to the advisor and the DSC schedule starts all over again. In some cases, the advisor simply doesn't disclose the fees, or they're disclosed but the advisor doesn't offer to rebate them, even when a rebate is allowed. Fortunately, with stricter regulations this type of abuse is getting harder for the unethical advisor to get away with.

Rebalancing may also trigger a switch fee. Such fees can fly under the compliance radar much easier. Most mutual fund companies allow unit holders to move between funds within the same fund family, and the same fee structure without paying a DSC. When processing such switches, many of the fund companies allow financial advisors to charge an optional switch fee of up to 2% to process the move. Clients can decline, but if the advisor doesn't tell them about it, they don't have that option. An advisor who has gone bankrupt could see this as a way to generate some quick cash, start rebalancing her clients' portfolios and charging this fee. Depending on her dealer, the advisor may be able to do this without disclosing the fee to the client. Or have an unsuspecting client simply sign a form without fully explaining what it is.

There's an even bigger problem concerning advisors who go bankrupt. The regulators who are supposed to protect clients don't require dealers to terminate, suspend or even increase supervision of an advisor when they declare bankruptcy. It's left up to individual dealers to decide how to handle such situations. Some dealers have a policy to terminate an advisor. Others won't. Some dealers will only allow the advisor to continue under strict supervision, in order to ensure the clients best interests are looked after.

If a dealer decides to terminate an advisor the advisor

may not be able to get sponsored by another dealer (MFDA or IIROC) until they emerge from bankruptcy. It could be argued this is a good thing as it eliminates the potential for a conflict of interest.

But even this may not keep them from putting clients at risk. If the advisor holds a life insurance license they could still sell insurance based investments. Remember the regulators are different and don't share information with each other. When one regulator makes a ruling the others aren't informed about it. This lack of integration between regulators essentially creates another opportunity for a conflict of interest.

For example, what's to stop an advisor who no longer holds a securities license (due to bankruptcy or some other reason) from contacting her previous clients and recommending they move to an insurance based investment? Nothing. And what about possible DSC fees to move? Where's the DSC fee disclosure? In this case there is none since the advisor is now selling through the unregulated MGA channel.

Clients faced with this situation may never know the real reason why they were advised to move. If full disclosure were required, they would at least have a chance to make an informed decision, with all the facts on the table.

For a client looking for a financial advisor, bankruptcy presents a potential conflict of interest and raises a major red flag. The advisor is under financial pressure because of the bankruptcy on the one hand and occupies a trusted position with access to his clients' money on the other. Unfortunately, the financial services industry in Canada does very little to protect the consumer from this risk. It's up to you, the client, to protect yourself against questionable recommendations from an advisor who may have gone bankrupt. So how do you do you check if your advisor has declared bankruptcy?

In Canada, it's relatively easy. You simply contact the Superintendent of Bankruptcy Canada, which is a federal government agency, by phone or online, pay a small fee and obtain a report that discloses basic information about anyone in this country who has declared bankruptcy, even past ones from which the person has been discharged.

You need to be specific about a person's name and their home address, which could be a problem if you don't know where they live or used to live. A person may even have declared bankruptcy in the past when he lived in a different city. You can still get the information, but you may have to pay for several reports applicable to different people with the same name. Fortunately, the reports cost less than $10.

Another option is to ask the advisors dealer firm if they are aware of any bankruptcies. Be prepared though, because of the dealers self interest in the advisor and the fees she can generate, they may be less than forthcoming about providing any information on this subject.

Figure 6: Office of the Superintendent of Bankruptcy Canada

National Headquarters phone: 613-941-1000
Website: www.ic.gc.ca/eic/site/bsf-osb.nsf/eng/home

Truth or dare: A conclusion to the advisor reference check

Wow, that was a lot of work, wasn't it? When it comes

down to it, there really is a lot of stuff to check out about a potential financial advisor. As if looking at the list of 13 items isn't enough, actually going through all the steps can be a daunting task.

The truth of the matter is, very few people will go through all the steps to complete a full Advisor Reference Check, not because it's not important or because they don't know what to do or how to do it – especially now that they have a step by step guide. It's just too much work. Even with the steps laid out this is very unfamiliar territory and it's just too complicated.

I'm in the business, I talk the language, and yet even I found it challenging to conduct a complete check the first time. So what's the answer? How else can you increase your chances of dealing with a true professional and reduce the possibility of becoming the victim of an unscrupulous advisor?

As I talked to a number of clients, colleagues and even friends about this issue, I wondered, What if there was a service that conducted this complete check for you? You could provide the basic information required, like the name, address and phone number of the advisor and the name of the firm she deals with. Then this company could go do all the legwork and provide a report listing all the key areas that were checked. It would look much like a home inspection report, but it would focus on the advisor and the dealer, not a house.

> The truth of the matter is, very few people will go through all the steps to complete a full Advisor Reference Check

This service would not make recommendations or referrals, and would make absolutely no judgments about the overall suitability of the advisor in the report. The report would simply deal with the facts as discovered through the reference checking process and present them to you.

The people I spoke with said they'd be far more likely to hire someone to do this than wade through all the bureaucracy by themselves. With such an enthusiastic response, I figured someone out there must already offer such a service, so I went on a search to find him. But the service I'd envisioned simply doesn't exist.

I did find a few companies that take various different approaches to helping consumers find a qualified advisor. Know Your Financial Advisor and Accretive Advisor, are two services offered in Canada, while the Paladin Registry offers a service in the USA. Below are links to their websites, as well as a brief description of each of these services.

Canadian Resource:
Know Your Financial Advisor: www.kyfa.com
Accretive Advisor: www.accretiveadvisor.com
US Resource:
Paladin Registry: www.paladinregistry.com

Know Your Financial Advisor

Know Your Financial Advisor (KYFA) is a web based service that offers a searchable database of licensed financial advisors from across Canada. Their goal is to help connect investors with advisors who can best fit their particular needs. As an investor you can search by location, specialty or by name.

The folks at Know Your Financial Advisor have done the research for the consumer. A basic listing on the KYFA site provides advisors names, their investment dealers name, along with their address and phone number. Where it differs from other online lists of advisors is that they provide unbiased, third party verification of a financial advisor's licenses, registrations and designations all in one place. Advisors can expand on this basic listing by providing information about their education, areas of specialization, fee structure and past work experience.

While this basic listing of an advisors credentials and licenses is a great first step, the real benefit to the consumer comes from something called the KYFA Trusted™ Badge. Under this "badge" is a much deeper level of scrutiny performed by KYFA. The additional verification isn't a one-time thing either. It's completed on an ongoing basis.

They check to see if the advisor is in good standing and committed to ongoing professional development with respect to their designations. When it comes to licenses they dig deeper to verify that the advisor has not been disciplined by the provincial securities commission or provincial insurance council. As for their registration with the self regulatory organization (SRO), they further verify that the advisor and his dealer are active and in good standing with their SRO. And finally they verify that the advisor has not been disciplined, paid or been ordered to pay any penalties or fines.

Keep in mind this additional level of due diligence isn't completed on all listed advisors. It's an optional service, chosen and paid for by the advisor. If a particular advisor isn't willing to pay for this service, you will still have to do the additional checking yourself. Alternatively you might consider only interviewing an advisor who is KYFA Trusted™.

Accretive Advisor

Accretive Advisor is another Canadian web based service to assist consumers in finding some of Canada's best financial advisors – or Elite advisors. Unlike KYFA, Accretive Advisor doesn't list all "registered" advisors in Canada. Accretive Elite is an unbiased program that recognizes and distinguishes some of Canada's best financial advisors for their service excellence to investors irrespective of what company they work for or under which regulator. Their process requires a qualifying advisor to survey their clients using their 360 Engagement Program: Client Audit. This tool is a way to gauge their current clients satisfaction with the service they provide.

In addition, Accretive does a detailed regulatory and compliance check on the advisor and does a business profile review by former industry professionals to ensure the advisor actually does what they say they do in their marketing material. If all checks out the advisor becomes an Accretive Elite advisor on the Accretive Advisor website. Investors can search for advisors under the investor section of the Accretive site. There they will find a selection of Elite advisors to select from and an intelligent search capability to find the one for them.

The Accretive Advisor site it free for the consumer, but advisors must pay to go through the certification process and be listed. Given the added costs for this service, there will likely be far fewer advisors listed. According to Accretive Advisor, they see this as an advantage because it allows them to have a listing of only Elite advisors in Canada. These two services are quite different. Therefore you may wish to give them both a try in your quest to find the best advisor match for your situation.

Paladin Registry

The Paladin Registry is designed to assist US based consumers find a professional financial advisor. According to their website, they focus on finding a "professional with the best qualifications, not the best sales pitch".

The Paladin Registry uses a number of metrics to rate advisors on a 5 Star rating system. Their pre-screening covers areas including: experience, education, certifications, compliance records and services offered. And not all advisors make the cut either.

Similar to Accretive Advisor, the Paladin Registry matches a consumers specific needs with the advisors qualifications to provide a list of pre-screened, documented financial professionals to choose from.

Conclusion

Before you move on to hiring your new advisor, you should take a moment to understand how advisors get paid. In the next chapter, I'll explain briefly the different ways in which advisors earn their living and clear up some misconceptions that people might have about fees and commissions.

Chapter 11: Fees, fees and more fees — what are they all for?

How financial advisors get paid is a mystery to most people. Some people even regard it as a taboo subject. Most would agree, though, that no one should work for free. On the other hand, if you don't know how much you're paying for a particular service or how the fees are being charged, you have a potential problem.

The financial services industry is under pressure to address this problem by disclosing in more detail the ways that clients pay for financial advice. I think this is a good thing. If it's done right, proper disclosure will benefit the buying public considerably. On the other hand overreacting to this problem could do more harm than good.

This problem around compensation and lack of disclosure sparked the debate that's going on in several countries at the time of writing this book. The question being considered is whether financial advisors should be held to a higher standard of care and be guided by a set of well-defined principles of conduct. Personally, I don't see the need for debate. All financial advisors should be held to a higher standard. I'll come back to this in a moment.

In the US there is a movement to apply something called the Fiduciary Standard to *all* financial professionals. The belief is that "such a move would presumably elevate the level of professionalism through law, to the extent that conflicts of interest around compensation would be very manageable". In the UK, by contrast, the Financial Services Authority (FSA) wants to ban commission-based compensation entirely. Similarly in Australia, the governing body for CFP™ professionals is considering prohibiting CFP™ practitioners from accepting commissions directly from any manufacturer of financial products. They would however be allowed to receive commissions after they are fully disclosed and accepted and signed off by their clients.

The problem isn't with commissions per se. The problem is with advisors who know how to abuse commissions for their own benefit, when dealing with clients who don't understand how commissions work. Such advisors have lots of opportunity to take advantage of their clients. And the clients will never know.

The average consumer is probably unaware that there is a duty of care in Canadian common law that all advisors are held to. This duty of care requires them to act fairly, honestly and in good faith in respect of their clients' interests. There are many professional advisors who understand this and take it to heart. The problem isn't with them. The problem is with the advisors who ignore this duty of care.

This duty of care is not the same as a Fiduciary Standard, but does cover most of the elements. I would argue that there may be some practical challenges to applying a Fiduciary Standard on advisors in Canada, which in the end may end up hurting more than helping the consumer.

In a practical sense, all advisors should at the very least be subject to the 5 principles that embody the Fiduciary Standard. I find it interesting that if you look closely you'll see that all 5 principles reflect

> **The problem isn't with commissions per se. The problem is with advisors who know how to abuse commissions for their own benefit, when dealing with clients who don't understand how commissions work.**

the spirit of the CFP™ Code of Ethics in its principles and rules. The 5 core principles of a Fiduciary (as described by the Committee for the Fiduciary Standard in the US) are:

1. Put the client's best interest first;

2. Act with prudence – that is, with the skill, care, diligence and good judgment of a professional;

3. Do not mislead clients – provide conspicuous, full and fair disclosure of all important facts;

4. Avoid conflicts of interest, and

5. Fully disclose and fairly manage, in the client's favor, unavoidable conflicts

This all sounds good in theory, but I'm sure you're wondering how this can help you?

As the old saying goes, "Knowledge is power." Now that you know advisors in Canada are held to a duty of care under common law, you can use this in your search when evaluating a new advisor. You can also use the principles of the Fiduciary Standard as they relate to the CFP® code of ethics to help guide your choice. This may mean only considering CFP® designated advisors who truly practice the principles of the CFP® code of Ethics.

When it comes to the topic of compensation, with a bit of understanding, you should be able to avoid the problems that are often associated with commissions and even take control of how your advisor is paid. This doesn't let the industry off the hook. It still needs to find better ways to ensure clients' best interests are addressed before the advisors' interests.

In the meantime, learning how advisors are paid is an important first step for you. So let's get down to learning the ins and outs of advisors' compensation.

Financial advisor compensation: The basics.

Financial advisors get compensated in four general ways:

1. Salary

2. Bonuses

3. Fees

4. Commissions

The way in which particular advisors get paid is sometimes a function of where they work. In other cases, the advisor decides how he will get paid, and this decision will be reflected in the way he sets up his company. For instance, most bank-based financial advisors are paid on salary with bonuses for hitting certain sales targets set by the bank. On the other hand, an independent, fee-only financial planner is paid a fee for the time he spends creating a financial plan.

Let's take a look at each of these options in more detail.

Salary + Bonus

This is the typical model found at most banks. Advisors in banks will most likely hold front-line sales positions. It's their job to sell their bank's mutual funds and deposit-based investments like GICs and CDs. Depending on how much money you have to invest, they may send you up the ladder to an in-house financial planner. At this level, you may get some basic financial planning advice and be offered the option of non-bank mutual funds, but with an emphasis on in-house products. Bank employees generally work on salary and qualify for bonuses based on sales targets set by the bank. In some cases, they may also receive commissions, although the customer may not know about them.

Things to watch out for:

Salary-based advisors usually work as employees of a bank or other financial institutions. This can lead to a conflict of interest, because they generally sell only the in-house products offered by their employer. If a client's situation calls for a product that the bank doesn't offer, the advisor generally won't recommend it, in many cases they can't. Salaried bank employees usually don't have the same level of vested interest in a client's success as an independent advisor, simply because they're limited in the advice and solutions they can offer.

Commission
Advisors who don't work for banks most commonly receive compensation in the form of commission. Basically, an advisor receives a commission upon the sale of a product or service, usually calculated as a percentage of the value of the transaction or sale. Commissioned advisors may work at a stock brokerage. They may also work for a mutual fund company or an insurance company or as independent financial planners working through a mutual fund dealer.

For the consumer, the challenge lies in figuring out which of many types of commission the advisor earns. Without knowing all the types and how they work, a client may end up with an advisor who is paid by commission and who puts his needs ahead of the client's.

Here is a brief summary of the different forms of commission in this industry:

Straight-up commission
The conventional stockbroker makes a living this way. He sells stuff and gets paid a direct commission based on the value of the sale. He gets paid when you buy an investment from him. And he gets paid again when you sell that investment later. If you don't buy and sell, he doesn't get paid.

Chapter 11: Fees, fees and more fees – what are they all for?

Things to watch out for:

It's easy for a broker to come back to the well periodically with a recommendation for a newer, better investment. Sometimes the broker may indeed have a legitimate reason to make the recommendation, but you need to keep in mind that it will cost money each time you sell an investment and buy another one. The challenge for the client is to know when a recommendation fits your needs rather than the broker's need to make a monthly payment on his Mercedes.

Front-end load (FEL)

This type of commission is associated with a mutual fund or segregated fund. The advisor charges you directly and up front when you purchase a fund, hence the name - front-end load (FEL).

This is perhaps the simplest, most transparent, yet least-used form of commission in the mutual fund world. Here's how it works. If you purchase $10,000 of the XYZ FUND you can negotiate the percentage commission you are willing to pay. That's right. I said "negotiate", which means you actually control the amount of commission you pay, within a range of 0% to 6%. You and your advisor agree on this commission before you make the purchase.

For example, if I negotiate a 3% commission, then I'll pay $300 on the purchase and it's deducted from my $10,000. So my net investment becomes $9,700. Right from the outset, I know my cost. After that, I can sell the fund without fees, commissions or penalties.

Most people don't know that they can negotiate this commission. They'd also be surprised to learn that they can purchase a FEL fund for 0% commission. That doesn't mean the advisor won't get paid. But instead of getting paid directly by you when you make the purchase, he receives his compensation in the form of a trailer fee from the fund company.

I'll explain later how trailer fees work.

Not all advisors will agree to a 0% commission, but those who work in their client's best interest will when circumstances require it. An FEL is sometimes called an initial sales charge (ISC), but it works the same way, by either name.

Things to watch out for:

Like a straight-up commission, an advisor can potentially take advantage of a client by selling mutual funds on a FEL basis. Because there are no fees to sell it, the advisor could keep coming back to the well, recommending periodically a newer, better fund. This is where you need to take control. If you paid a commission the first time the money was invested, and if there's a legitimate reason to switch to a new fund, you should make the switch on a 0% basis. After all, why should an advisor get paid more than one commission on the same money, when she's earning a trailer fee as well?

Deferred sales charge (DSC)

A deferred sales charge may be applied to the purchase of a mutual fund or segregated fund. It's probably the most common form of commission and the one that causes the most grief for the average investor. Unlike the front-end load, you don't pay anything up front when you buy a fund this way. If you invest $10,000 in a fund on a DSC basis, the full $10,000 gets invested. The commission is paid to the advisor by the fund company, not by you. The standard industry commission is 5%, and it is paid to the advisor's dealer. The dealer takes a cut, and the balance is paid to the advisor.

So far, so good.

The deferred part of the fee comes into play at the back end, when you take money out of the fund. Remember, the fund company paid your advisor a commission when you bought the investment. To make that commission back, the company must keep your money invested for a certain period. If you take out your money before the company has recovered its costs, it will charge you a fee. This is called a deferred sales charge.

As time goes by, the fund company makes money on your money, and the deferred sales charge decreases. Most fund companies apply a DSC on a declining scale over 6 or 7 years. After that, the company no longer charges you a fee to get your money out.

> It's probably the most common form of commission and the one that causes the most grief for the average investor.

For example, if you purchase a fund with a 6-year declining DSC, you may pay 6% if you cash in your investment in year one, 5% in year two and 1% in the 6th year. In the 7th year, you no longer have to pay a fee.

With this type of commission, you pay nothing out of your own pocket when you invest, and the advisor earns the money she needs to do the work that you've hired her to do. A DSC arrangement also works for clients who don't want to pay their advisor a direct fee for creating a financial plan, as long as the clients purchase their investments from the person who creates the plan. This way, the advisor gets compensated indirectly from the fund company for doing the planning work for you.

At first glance, this might seem like an ideal arrangement. Under certain circumstances, it is. But you need to invest your money and leave it invested until the DSC schedule runs out. If you think you'll need money before the DSC schedule runs out, your advisor should direct at least some of you money to a fund that does not apply a DSC. As always, you also need to deal with an ethical advisor.

Things to watch out for:
One problem with a DSC fund is that it restricts your access to your own money. Putting everything in a DSC fund might make sense when you do it. But life happens and situations change, and you may need your money before the DSC schedule expires. As years pass, clients sometimes forget about the fee involved with money invested in a DSC fund. Just when you need the money, you're reminded of the fee, which means you have less at your disposal than you thought. With some simple planning, you can avoid this problem.

For instance, allocating some of your money to a 0% FEL fund can reduce or eliminate this problem. You can make this allocation at the outset or take advantage of the annual fee-free switches offered by most mutual fund companies. With a fee-free switch, most DSC funds allow you to withdraw 10% of the value of your investment each year without paying a fee. If you take full advantage of this option and move 10% of your investment to a FEL version of the fund, you should make sure that you do it for a 0% commission or that your advisor doesn't charge you a switch fee to move it.

The biggest problem with DSC funds arises when an advisor doesn't fully explain how the DSC arrangement works. Sometimes advisors don't discuss it at all. Regulators and dealers insist on disclosure at the time of sale, yet many advisors who use DSC funds don't discuss commissions or how they get paid. They may simply say, "Don't worry. The fund company pays me to invest your money. It won't cost you anything." The advisor will then ask you to sign the application and some other papers, provide you with a prospectus, and this will satisfy the dealer and the regulator. Now you're the owner of a DSC fund, with a potential fee time-bomb ticking away.

Another problem arises when an advisor recommends a change in investments and moves the money to a new fund company. If the DSC schedule hasn't expired, you'll pay a fee. Sometimes an advisor sees a legitimate reason for making such a change, and the fee makes sense. But this doesn't necessarily mean you have to pay it. If you're dealing with an ethical advisor, she'll remind you of the fee and discuss your options for paying it.

Options, you say?

You can pay this fee if the change makes sense and you are willing to pay it. If you do pay it, you'll want to negotiate a 0% FEL on the new investment, as I mentioned earlier, so you don't have to pay yet another fee. Remember, if you've invested in a DSC fund, the fund company has already paid your advisor a commission on the money. In many cases, when doing a switch like this, the new fund company allows advisors to offer you a fee rebate. This way, the fee is paid for you. Here's how it works.

Let's say I've been invested in a mutual fund for 5 years, and my fee to get out is now 2%. If I want this fee rebated, my advisor can purchase the new investment on a DSC basis, which generates a new commission. Some or all of this new commission is then used by the new fund company to rebate the fees that I paid to get out of the first fund.

If done properly, you and your advisor sign a fee-rebate form, and your advisor tells you in detail how the new DSC arrangement works.

The downside is that your new fund comes with a new DSC schedule that will extend over another 6 or 7 years. Your advisor may continue to move your money every few years into another DSC fund and offer each time to rebate the fees. You won't pay the fees, but you'll never get out of a DSC schedule. Fortunately, there's a way around this, too. After all, you probably won't want to keep your money in a DSC fund perpetually, nor should your advisor get paid over and over again on the same money.

First, your advisor needs to determine the fee involved to get out of the fund. Then she can purchase just enough of the new fund on a DSC basis to pay the fee completely. The remaining money goes into a 0% FEL fund. This way your fee gets paid, and you don't tie up all of your money in a new DSC fund.

Segregated investment funds offered by insurance companies can also be sold on a FEL or DSC basis. But unlike mutual funds, insurance regulators don't allow rebates on

DSC fees charged by segregated fund companies. If your insurance advisor wants to move funds around before the DSC schedule is over, and you agree to do so, beware that you will have to pay the fees. This is one more reason why Segregated Funds should be regulated under the MFDA and IIROC.

Whenever an advisor moves money from one DSC fund to another or from a FEL fund to a DSC fund, the advisor could be churning your investment. This means she gets paid commissions over and over again on the same money.

Advisors can also churn your money when a fund's DSC schedule expires. Once there's no longer a fee involved, some advisors will move your money into another fund with a new DSC schedule. This way they get paid again, and the client gets locked into another schedule of fees.

In an attempt to protect clients, some mutual fund dealers now require advisors and clients to sign a DSC and commission disclosure form whenever an advisor recommends such a move. This signed form is supposed to ensure that clients know they're locking themselves into a new DSC schedule and approve of the new commission paid to the advisor.

As the old saying goes, where there's a will, there's a way. Assuming the advisor holds both a mutual funds license and an insurance license, she can take an unethical way around this disclosure form. For example, the advisor can move a client's investment from a mutual fund that has an expired DSC schedule into a segregated fund offered by an insurance company sold through their MGA.

Remember, mutual funds and segregated funds are regulated by two entirely distinct regimes. Rules that apply to one don't apply to the other. Insurance advisors who sell segregated funds through an MGA operate virtually without regulation. There is no such thing as a DSC disclosure form in the insurance side of the business. Sure, the advisor must provide an information folder that accompanies the investment once it is sold, but that's about it. The exception to this is where an advisor sells Segregated Funds through his investment dealer, either MFDA or IIIROC. In that case they will be subject to all the normal regulatory requirements and disclosure rules.

> Used properly, DSC can allow access to financial planning that many clients may otherwise not get.

As massive numbers of boomers near retirement, I suspect this kind of activity will happen more frequently. Boomers want guaranteed income, and coincidently the insurance industry is heavily promoting segregated funds with a Guaranteed Living Income Benefits (GLIB). For the unethical advisor, this presents an opportunity to churn their clients' mutual funds. Preying on their clients' concerns, they can recommend a wonderful new product that will guarantee a minimum level of income, with upside potential to earn even more. They can't offer this with a mutual fund.

Insurance companies promote these products as private pensions and income plans. According to their logic, you won't want to cash out of them, but hold them for the long term so you can collect the income. The unethical advisor sees this as a reason to sell you such a fund on a DSC basis. But if a DSC schedule has already matured on your investment in a mutual fund, for which the advisor has already been paid, why not purchase the 0% FEL version of the segregated fund?

Sure, the regulators say they've clamped down, and mutual fund dealers say they have systems in place to prevent advisors from lining their pockets at your expense, but they can still do it. These shenanigans happen far more often than you might think, but they don't have to happen to you. If you know what to look for and put together a couple of simple questions, you can prevent the abuses of DSC.

Used properly, DSC can allow access to financial planning that many clients may otherwise not get. At the same time, DSC enables an ethical advisor to get paid properly for providing that planning and solid financial advice.

Fee for Service and Fee-Based Compensation

Financial advisors may also get compensated through fees, which work much differently than commissions. Some critics of commission-based selling say the whole industry should move toward a strictly fee-based structure.

Advisors earn fees in two distinct ways: fee for service and fee-based compensation.

Fee for Service

Your lawyer or accountant usually earns a fee for service, getting paid for his time and advice. In a similar way, a fee-for-service advisor/planner charges a fee to perform a specific service usually based on the time required to do the job. An advisor may charge $200 per hour, for example, or she may charge a flat rate of $1,500 to complete a specific job, regardless of how long it takes.

Financial advisors may charge a fee for service for a number of different services. The two most common services are: to evaluate an investment portfolio and recommend changes, and to create a written financial plan. Under this structure, the advisor receives no compensation for the sale of any product, just a set fee for evaluation and advice.

Fee Based

An advisor earns fee-based compensation for managing a client's financial assets rather than completing a specific job. A fee-based advisor charges an annual advisory fee, specified in advance, to manage the client's financial assets and provides ongoing advice as part of that role. Some traditional stock brokers have moved to this model.

A fee-based advisor generally uses different types of investments than a commissioned advisor to meet a client's needs. These investments may come with no embedded fees. Or if they do have embedded fees, they will generally be lower than a comparable investment offered by a commission based advisor. A true fee-based advisor will not earn income from commissions on the sale of investments.

For instance, a fee-based advisor may invest on behalf of a client in an F-Class mutual fund that carries a management fee of 0.75%. (F-Class stands for fee based) The advisor may then charge an advisory fee of 1% to manage the client's assets and provide ongoing advice. The client pays a total fee of 1.75%.

By comparison, a person who buys the same mutual fund (but a non F-Class version) from a commission based advisor pays no fee directly to the advisor. The mutual fund company will charge a higher management fee in the range of 1.75% - 3% (This depends on the fund company and the amount invested). From that management fee the advisor will receive his compensation as a trailer fee. This trailer fee is to the commission based advisor, what the advisory fee is to the fee-based advisor.

Obviously the fees charged by a fee-based advisor are potentially lower. I say potentially, because this will depend on the fee that the advisor charges directly for her services and on the embedded fee in the comparable commission based product.

In the previous example, if the fee-based advisor charged 1.25% on his fund with the .75% embedded fee, and the management fee in the fund chosen by the commission based advisor is 2%, then the client would pay exactly the same. The only difference is that the fee-based advisor's compensation is not related to a "commission based product", but is charged directly to the client. For this reason, some people incorrectly assume that a fee-based advisor gives more objective advice. This is not necessarily the case.

Why doesn't everyone choose a fee based advisor?

First, there are far fewer fee-based advisors in the industry, so it's more difficult to find one. Second, most fee-based advisors place a minimum size on the accounts that they'll manage. Some will manage accounts no smaller than $1 million. Others may accept accounts as small as $250,000. The advisor bases these self-imposed minimums on the amount of income that she needs to generate from each account to make a profit. If your account doesn't meet the minimum to qualify, this type of advisor will not accept you as a client.

If you still prefer a fee-based model, you may find an advisor who uses what I call a *hybrid* fee based compensation model. In this model they earn compensation mainly from trailer fees, and who will accept you as a client without a large minimum account size.

I'll talk about these fees in the next section.

Trailer Fees

Commission-based advisors earn part of their income in the form of a commission called a trailer fee. The advisor receives this fee on a monthly basis from a mutual fund company in return for managing his client's accounts.

The advisor receives a trailer fee whether you purchase a mutual fund that comes with a front-end load (FEL) or a deferred sales charge (DSC). On a DSC fund, though, the fund company pays a smaller trailer fee because the advisor earns a commission at the outset. On a FEL fund, the trailer fee is usually twice as large, because the advisor doesn't earn a commission upfront from the fund company.

Trailer fees were originally intended to compensate advisors for providing ongoing services to their clients. While they are technically considered a commission, trailer fees can also contribute to a hybrid of the fee-based compensation model.

As I mentioned, many fee-based advisors accept clients only with accounts of a minimum size, because they can't make a profit on smaller accounts. Yet everyone should have access to good professional advice, no matter how much money she has. Such advice is available from professional advisors who use a commission-based compensation model in an ethical manner.

The hybrid model

In general, an advisor does most of her work when a client first engages her services. For a fee-based advisor with a large minimum account size, the fee will generally cover the cost of this work over time. But smaller accounts can't generate the same level of fees.

Those people with smaller accounts may have no choice. Since many fee-based advisors won't accept them as clients, they may have to work with a commission based advisor to get access to professional planning. The alternative is to create their own plan and invest themselves through an online discount brokerage account or a bank, without the benefit of ongoing professional advice. And unless they hire a fee-for-service planner to create a financial plan, they won't get advice on the important areas of tax, insurance, cash-flow, risk management and estate planning

To overcome this challenge some commission based advisors offer a *hybrid model* using regular mutual funds or segregated funds. These types of investments come with a management fee. Part of this fee compensates the advisor through an embedded trailer fee paid directly to the advisor. Because of these trailer fees, the management fee on a mutual fund purchased through a commission-based advisor is higher than the same fund purchased through a fee based advisor using F-Class funds.

In order to get compensated for this early work on the smaller accounts, a commission-based advisor could use DSC funds for some of a client's investments, receiving a commission from the fund company for this upfront work, and use 0% FEL funds for the rest of the client's investments. After that, as I discussed earlier, the advisor can use the 10% fee-free switch option to transfer the client's money gradually from the DSC fund to a FEL fund. Once all of the client's money is moved to a FEL fund, the commission-based advisor generally receives a trailer fee of up to 1% to reimburse him for ongoing services and advice.

> **Everyone should have access to good professional advice, no matter how much money she has.**

There are some commission based advisors whose *hybrid model* uses only FEL 0% funds paying them the 1% trailer and they never sell DSC funds at all. No matter how they eventually get to the 1% trailer, this fee amounts to about the same as most fee-based advisors charge their clients directly. When using a commission-based advisor, the client pays higher overall fees and the advisor is paid indirectly by the fund company.

Insurance Industry: Bonuses and Perks

For the most part bonuses and perks for financial advisors, based on sales production has been eliminated from the investment industry in Canada. Companies can no longer offer incentives for using their particular product over another. This is a good thing, as it helps to better align the interests of the client to the product solution being offered.

Unfortunately this is not the case in the insurance industry in Canada. Sales contests with expensive prizes and conferences in exotic locations are still the norm in this sector of the financial services industry. Many insurance companies offer annual or bi-annual conferences for agents selling their product. In order to qualify the agent has to place a certain quantity of business (usually a large quantity) with that company during the qualifying period. If they do, they are rewarded with an all expenses paid trip or cruise to the conference. The conference is often times less about business and more about recreation and reward for using that company's products.

Why is it a problem? This is a huge potential conflict of interest that puts clients at risk. An insurance advisor, who chooses to do so, can use this system to qualify for any conference of their choice. To do this they need only sell a particular companies product to the majority of clients during the qualifying period, even if it isn't the right or best product for the client at the right time. Some insurance advisors even rotate which company conference they want to attend from year to year. Some advisors do something called "sandbagging". This is where they hold off on making recommendations to clients until the contest begins. That way the sales will come in during the qualification period. This is major conflict of interest especially when dealing with insurance products that could be time sensitive. Advisors that do this, do so with little if any regard for their client's best interest.

Other contests happen from time to time as a way for an insurance company or managing general agency (MGA) to boost their sales numbers of a certain product. For instance, incentives like – big screen TVs, laptop computers and iPads will be offered to advisors with the top number of sales for a particular product. Cross sell contests are also very popular with insurance companies. For example, they'll offer prizes for advisors to sell a bunch of critical illness insurance to all the clients they have previously sold life insurance to – hence the "cross sell".

To some this may appear to be a legitimate way to motivate advisors to sell products to clients who need them. For the ethical advisor this may be true. However, the time to sell a particular product to a client should be based on when they need it, not when an advisor needs another sale to win a contest or qualify for a convention.

Unfortunately the motivation to win these prizes can cloud some advisors judgment, and clients might get talked into something they really don't need. This is why, like their counterparts in the investment industry, all such perks, conferences and bonuses should be banned in the insurance industry. It's interesting to note the proposed ban on commissions in England had more to do with incentive based sales of insurance products, than it did with problems around commissions on the sale of investments.

Summary

While there is clearly room for abuse of commissions by some advisors, I believe getting rid of it entirely will hurt far more clients than it will help. Critics argue that a universal fee-based model is the only way to eliminate abuse. They argue that, if a client wants advice, he can eliminate any potential conflict of interest by paying an advisor directly for that advice. Paying for advice this way cannot ensure the elimination of conflicts altogether.

> **Transaction-oriented advisors are most likely to abuse the commission system and work in their best interests, not yours.**

There are a couple of serious problems with this proposed solution. First of all, the average consumer is not yet willing to write a cheque out of his own pocket to pay for this type of advice. Business owners and high net worth clients may be willing to do so as they're already used to paying directly for advice. But for the average consumer, given the choice, if they really understood how their advisor is paid and they judged it as fair, most would rather their advisors be paid by the fund companies.

Secondly, if commissions (including trailer fees) were eliminated tomorrow there would likely be a mass exodus of advisors out of the industry. With their primary source of income being eliminated, and consumers not yet willing to pay the fees directly, how could they afford to stay in business? By the way this wouldn't just eliminate the unethical advisor.

Even if commission-based advice was eliminated, the quality of advice would not necessarily improve nor would conflicts of interest disappear. In the meantime, while this is all being considered, clients with accounts too small to meet a fee-based advisor's minimum size would be left stranded. They may have financial planning needs as complicated as anyone else's, but they'd have nowhere to turn for help.

Certainly the industry must clean up the abuses of commission-based selling, and get rid of perks and bonuses in the insurance industry. Applying the 5 Core Principles of a Fiduciary to all financial advisors may be part of the solution. In the meantime, you can use the information I've provided about advisor compensation to protect yourself.

More important, you need to find a planning-based advisor who focuses on more than individual transactions. Transaction-oriented advisors are most likely to abuse the commission system and work in their best interests, not yours.

We'll deal with this topic in more detail in the next chapter.

Chapter 12: Planning or transaction focused?

Whether you've checked out prospective advisors on your own or found a service to do some of the work for you, you're ready to move on to the very last step in hiring your new advisor. Once he has passed the acid test and you've found a legitimate advisor with a clear record, you now have to find out if he's truly planning focused or if he's transaction focused.

You might wonder about the difference between a planning focused advisor and a transaction focused advisor. In a nutshell, an advisor who's transaction focused will likely discuss only investments. Over time lots of transactions will take place, buying, selling, buying some more. The advisor will likely make lots of commissions and trading fees, and you will pay them. There will be little if any discussion about how to generate lifelong, sustainable and guaranteed income. There likely won't be any tax planning, and as for product allocation, well let's just say that concept is usually foreign to a transaction-oriented advisor.

As discussed earlier, this is the old-school focus of a traditional stock-broker.

If you're going to make the transition to retirement successfully, you don't need a transaction-focused advisor. You need a professional planner who's on the same page as you, who focuses on retirement income planning.

So how can you tell the difference between transaction and planning focused advisor before you hire one? You can ask a series of questions during your initial interview.

Interview? What interview?

Eventually you have to sit down for a face-to-face meeting with one or two prospective advisors. At this point you can ask some very specific questions to determine how the advisor would handle your financial requirements. Many advisors will try to take charge of this meeting and dazzle you with facts and figures about themselves. Some will try to get a bunch of information about you and, more specifically, about how much money you have to invest with them. You just have to dig in your heels, put on the brakes and take charge of the meeting.

When you make the initial call to meet with an advisor you should make it very clear what you expect this first meeting to be about. At this first meeting, you're interested more in determining if the advisor fits your needs than in reassuring the advisor that your investment assets fit his business. Tell the advisors that they were recommended and that you've already completed a thorough background check on them (assuming you've done so). Make it known that you'll be asking them for information on the kind of clients they specialize in, specifics about their business model and processes, details on the services they provide and full and plain disclosure of how they're compensated.

You may not feel like a professional interviewer or know what questions you should ask? So I've provided some help.

Answers to these general questions will provide basic insights into an advisor's business. Keep in mind that if you've done the complete Financial Advisor Check discussed in Chapter 10, you'll already have the answers to some of these questions. Some people, however, might prefer to do this interview before doing the full Financial Advisor Check. It really doesn't matter which one you do first. What is important is that you do both!

Some organizations recommend asking a prospective advisor a series of questions before deciding to hire them. Below is a list of these traditional questions you might ask.

Traditional Sample Interview Questions:

1. What is your educational background?

2. What licenses do you hold?

3. What products do you sell?

4. Who is your investment dealer?

5. Have you ever had any disciplinary action against you from your dealer or a regulatory governing body?

6. Do you have any official professional designations?

7. Do you provide financial planning services?

8. How long have you been in the business?

9. Do you specialize in working with a specific type of client?

10. How many clients do you have?

11. Do you work with a partner, associate, or junior advisor?

12. Will you be doing the work on my account, or will someone else?

13. Do you have a business continuation plan in place should something happen to you?

14. What specific services do you provide?

15. How often can I expect to meet with you if you take me on as a client?

16. How are you compensated? Fee only, commission, hourly?

17. Why do you feel you are someone I can trust with my money?

These questions are a good starting point, yet most of them don't get to the heart of the difference between a transaction-based advisor versus a planning-oriented advisor. To determine this, you need to ask some more pointed questions about the advisor's processes and his approach to dealing with clients.

The next questionnaire is called the Planning Report Card. It's interesting to note that, like the Financial Advisor Checklist, this too came directly from discussions with clients. At the time I came up with this, we had just met for an initial review meeting after a seminar. In that meeting, this couple said that they were having difficulty trying to judge or compare the services of the advisors they were considering. One of them said it was too bad that financial advisors didn't have some kind of report card like the one kids get in school. She was, of course, a retired teacher.

That's when the Planning Report Card was born. It's a simple tool in the form of a questionnaire that you can use to find out exactly how a financial advisor approaches his clients with respect to planning. The questions are based on the principles of planning and a client-centred approach. One of the goals of this questionnaire is to determine if a specific planner is actually planning focused. But it provides much more than that.

Almost all of the questions can be answered with yes or no. If you find that an advisor answers no to most of the questions about planning, compensation and servicing, then it may be time to move on to another candidate.

The Planning Report Card is broken into sections that group pertinent information together for ease of evaluation. The five sections of the questionnaire are:

Financial Planning Services, Compensation Disclosure, Practice Management, Investment Management Services, and *Regulatory Issues.*

Here are the questions, with some elaboration on a few of the more uncommon ones. For a printable copy of the questionnaire, go to www.FearlessRetirementResources.com.

Financial Planning Services

1. Do you use a Letter of Engagement that outlines all the pertinent details of the work you agree to do? *(This is a requirement for a CFP™)*

2. Do you offer both segmented and comprehensive financial planning services? *(Segmented plans are for a single goal like education or retirement, comprehensive covers all aspects of a person's financial life)*

3. Do you specialize in a specific category of planning – i.e. retirement income planning, estate planning, investment planning or tax planning?

4. When beginning the financial planning process, do you use a comprehensive documents checklist or questionnaire to ensure you have a total picture and overview of a clients complete financial situation?

5. Do you use some form of values checklist or goals questionnaire to determine what is truly important to your clients as it relates to money?

6. Do you provide a detailed risk analysis showing all the potential risks that your client's situation is exposed to?

7. Do you provide a comprehensive written analysis of your client's financial situation, including various recommendations?

8. Do you offer assistance with implementation of the plan?

9. If not, do you have a referral arrangement in place with other professionals and are you compensated in some way for those referrals?

10. Do you offer continuous ongoing monitoring and advice related to the implementation of the plan?

11. Do you provide estate planning services for your clients including a review of critical estate documents such as wills and powers of attorney?

12. If so do you offer to coordinate the estate plan with other professionals involved, such as accountants and lawyers?

13. Do you provide risk management planning, including life, critical illness and long term care insurance?

Compensation
1. How are you compensated?
   Fee only?
   Hourly fee for service?
   Flat fee?
   Commissions only; from securities, insurance, annuities, GIC's, CD's etc?
   Fee and commission?
2. If you earn commissions, approximately what percentage do you earn from each product category listed below? *(The answer to this question will give you a good indication of whether the advisor uses a product allocation approach, especially if the advisor doesn't use Annuities, GMWB's, GIC's or CD's.)*

Mutual Funds	_____%
Segregated Funds	_____%
Annuities	_____%
GMWB products	_____%
GIC's or CD's	_____%
Limited Partnerships	_____%
Stocks	_____%
Bonds	_____%

3. Do you receive ongoing compensation in the form of trailers from the mutual funds, pooled funds, or

segregated funds that you sell?
4. Do you have a minimum fee or a minimum investment required?
5. Are there any financial incentives for you to recommend certain financial products over others? If so, what are they?
6. Do you offer to pay rebates in situations where a DSC fee is involved because of a transaction you have recommended?
7. Do you receive referral fees from other professionals – such as mortgage brokers, accountants, lawyers, insurance agents?
8. Do you provide complete written disclosure of your compensation prior to a client making an investment?
9. Do you have a written agreement as part of your letter of engagement that outlines all the ways in which you are compensated?

Practice Management
1. Do you provide complete written disclosure of all your business relationships, potential conflicts of interest, and a complaint resolution process at the beginning of your client engagement?
2. Do you meet with your clients at least annually to update their overall financial plan? *(This is separate from an investment review meeting and is designed to determine how much follow up or monitoring of the plan is done.)*

3. Do you meet with your clients at least annually to do a complete investment review to determine where the investments are relative to where the investment plan projected them to be?
4. Are you available by phone or email whenever needed (within reason)?
5. Do you have staff members who will handle certain components of our relationship – such as administrative duties etc?
6. Do you review your clients' stated and documented expectations of you and your services at least once per year?
7. Do you review your clients' tax returns on an annual basis to ensure they are paying the least amount of tax possible, at least with respect to the investments they have?

Investment Management Services
1. As part of your investment recommendations, do you use an Investment Policy Statement that clearly shows how and why the particular investments chosen meet the client's risk tolerance, time horizon, and stated goals including income requirement?
2. If you were to handle my account, do your require discretionary trading authority?
(If they do require it, this could be considered a red flag as it allows them to move funds whenever they wish. Having such power may allow them to generate income for themselves whenever they wish. A yes answer for this question should be considered a red flag)

3. Before making investment recommendations, do you always take your clients through a detailed risk assessment process to determine their comfort level with types of investments and their associated risks?
4. Do you use a product allocation model when designing an overall investment plan? *(Answering no to this question will be a good indication that the advisor is not focused on retirement income planning.)*

Regulatory Issues
1. Is your firm a member of an SRO, and if so which one?
2. Does your firm have an internal compliance process and department in place?
3. Is your business subject to regular third party compliance audits? If so when was your last audit?
4. Does someone besides you oversee and approve the trades you do for your clients?
5. Do you have current error and omission (E&O) insurance in force and how much is it?
6. Do you belong to a financial planning association and which one?
7. Are you an active member of that association in good standing?
8. Do you complete more than just the minimum continuing education requirements to maintain your various designations? If so, how many hours do you complete in an average year? _____

The Done-For-You Interview

As with completing the Financial Advisor Check, this interview can take some time and effort. It's quite likely that few people will be comfortable enough or even willing to do it on their own. Without the answers to these questions, though, it will be nearly impossible to know up front whether an advisor is planning focused or transaction oriented. This is critical information for you to know. So if you're not willing to do this level of interview, how can you get the answers you need?

What if someone did the interview for you?

That was the question my clients asked after I'd discussed this issue with them. In addition to having the Financial Advisor Checklist done for them, they suggested that having someone else ask these interview questions would be preferred. Just like with the financial advisor checking service, I couldn't find a company that offers such a service.

The closest thing to having this interview done is to use one of the advisor matching resources I mentioned in chapter 10. As a reminder, they are:

Know Your Financial Advisor: www.kyfa.com
Accretive Advisor: www.accretiveadvisor.com
Paladin Registry www.paladinregistry.com
(USA resource)

These services don't ask the specific questions found in the Planning Report Card. If you use one of them, you won't necessarily determine if an advisor is planning focused or transaction focused. You will however gain a better understanding of the advisors approach.

Chapter 13: Mixing psychology with math to create your retirement income plan

Up to this point, I've discussed the various risks you'll likely face in retirement. I introduced you to the simple **Four Planning Cornerstone** approach to retirement income planning. We discussed the psychology of matching your retirement income to your expenses with the **Retirement Spending Funnel** based on Maslow's hierarchy of needs. I also gave you the tools to document your income and expenses with the income/expense worksheet, and your assets with the asset worksheet. Finally, we took a field trip to a mathematics lab to learn about a new way to consider positioning your pot of gold called **product allocation** and its importance to your future.

For those who would rather work with a financial advisor, I gave you a set of tools to help hire the right one.

It's now time to bring all these elements together and put theory into action. Don't worry, I promised to keep this simple and I keep my promises. In this section of the book I'll show you exactly how to create your own retirement income plan. This means you have some work to do.

By combining your data from the Income/Expense and Asset Worksheets with the Retirement Spending Funnel, you'll know what you'll likely spend in retirement, because you will have listed and prioritized it. You'll also be able to set up the required separate pots of money to produce the lifetime income you need by using my **Funding Matrix**, which I'll introduce in this chapter.

> **In this section of the book I'll show you exactly how to create your own retirement income plan. This means you have some work to do.**

For those of you who don't work with a financial advisor, this will be the key you've been looking for. But because you're not working with an advisor you'll also have a little extra work to do in this section. Keep in mind, once your plan is complete you'll still need to find someone to sell you some of the products required to put the plan into action.

If you are working with a financial advisor, you may wonder why the advisor doesn't do this work for you. Some good, qualified advisors specialize in this area, and yours may be one of them. But not all financial advisors specialize in creating retirement income plans. Furthermore, few will know about the simple tools I'll show you or how to use them. Before you sit down with your advisor, you can use these tools to create your own plan. You'll gain a clearer understanding of your needs, so you can better articulate them to your advisor. After all, it's your financial security we're talking about. Having a better understanding of your situation and being on the same page as your advisor can only be of benefit to you.

If your advisor is well versed in this area of planning, she'll quite likely appreciate your initiative and involvement.

If not, being armed with a simple plan and a clear understanding of your needs, you'll be able to help your advisor in selecting the products that are most beneficial to you. In the worst case, you may find that it's time to find a new advisor, who understands the mechanics of retirement income planning. If that's the case, chapters 10, 11 and 12 showed you how to do that.

First Things First

What follows is a simple step-by-step guide to building your Retirement Income Plan. I've designed this as a fill-in-the-blanks process. Once you complete it, you will have your very own plan. For this to work you'll need the two worksheets discussed earlier in the book. You'll also find two additional worksheets in this chapter.

What You Need:

1. Completed Income and Expense Worksheet

2. Completed Available Assets Worksheet

3. A blank copy of the Retirement Spending Funnel

4. A blank copy of the Funding Matrix

All of these materials can be found in Appendix 3 of the book. Or you can download full-size copies from www.fearlessretirementresources.com.

This chapter includes examples and brief case studies of common situations that boomers might face. The examples illustrate the concept of **product allocation** in general and in conjunction with the concept of the **Retirement Spending Funnel**. Please keep in mind that the specific product recommendations are just examples, based on fictitious people. They may not be appropriate for all situations. When you apply the product allocation model to your own situation, you can choose from many different combinations of products.

As always, it's important to consult a qualified and licensed financial professional (preferably a Certified Financial Planner®) when considering specific products for yourself. You should not apply recommendations in these case studies to your own unique situation, nor should you interpret them as investment advice. They're just examples.

Step 1: Determine your Expenses & Guaranteed Income
If you haven't already done it, fill in all your income and expense numbers in the **Income/Expense Worksheet**. Keep in mind that the more detailed you are, the more accurate your plan. I've tried to include a comprehensive list of categories in this worksheet. But don't limit yourself to my list. If you spend money on something that's not on the list, be sure to include it under Other. If you have Esteem Expenses or Legacy Expenses/Gifts, be sure to include them in the appropriate section of the worksheet.

What income numbers should you use?
At this point some of you may wonder what income numbers to use and where to find them. This depends on whether

Chapter 13: Mixing psychology with math to create your retirement income plan 209

you're already retired or not. If you're retired you'll find this task a little easier. Remember, at this point, you're looking specifically for guaranteed sources of income, not variable income from your investments. We'll get to income from investments later, when you start to allocate your products.

With respect to your income numbers, it's important that you use NET amounts. What do I mean by that? Net amounts refer to the amount of income that you actually deposit to your bank account, after income tax, and that's available for you to spend. We can't avoid paying income tax. However, when and how we pay our taxes can vary from person to person. You need to consider your situation and how you deal with taxes.

With respect to income from government and private pensions and other sources, for example, some people have taxes withheld at source, meaning they get a net amount in their bank account. Others have no tax withheld and have to pay a tax bill every year. Do you pay your income taxes at source or once a year at tax time?

If you're one of the **retired folks**, you'll use the income numbers that you receive from the following sources:
- Government pensions: CPP & OAS if you're Canadian and Social Security if you're American
- Workplace pension
- Annuity income
- Any other source of guaranteed income

If you receive a net amount after taxes have been withheld, use that number. If you don't have taxes withheld, use the gross income you receive, but don't forget to enter your annual taxes under Basic Expenses to calculate your net income. The best place to get these numbers is from your bank statement and tax return.

If you're still working, this task will be a little more difficult, since you're creating a plan for your future retirement income, not the current income you receive from work. So where do you get the numbers for your potential guaranteed sources of income at retirement?

- If you have a work pension, you should receive an annual estimate of your expected pension upon retirement. If you can't find it, your employer's human resources department can provide it.
- If you expect to qualify for a government pension, you can contact the appropriate government agency to get an estimate of the amount. For additional resources go to www.yourfearlessretirementresources.com.
- If you're close to retirement and have purchased a deferred annuity, you should know how much you'll receive and when the payments will start. Include this amount under annuities.
- If you have any other guaranteed sources of income that will start when you retire, you should include them in the appropriate section.

Based on your expected gross incomes your next task is to estimate your income taxes and enter that number in the basic expenses section. Naturally taxes depend on the level of income and where you live. You can estimate average tax rates using government websites in your country. Or go to www.fearlessretirementresources.com for a list of resources.

Step 2: Determine what Investment Assets you have to use
If you haven't already done so, fill in the **Available Assets Worksheet**. This is where you will list all the investments you've accumulated over the years. They should include all your **_retirement accounts_** such as: RRSPs, RRIFs, LIRAs, LIFs, IRAs, 401(K)s, TFSA's and Roth IRA's. If you have a Defined Contribution (DC) pension plan at work, don't forget to include it here with your retirement accounts.

To qualify as a retirement account it must be tax sheltered *and/or* tax deferred, meaning you won't pay tax on the investment until you withdraw money from the account. When you do withdraw money, it is generally fully taxed as income in the year received. Exceptions to this are: Tax Free Savings Accounts (TFSA) in Canada and Roth IRA's in the USA. These plans are generally tax sheltered, but the withdrawls are not taxed.

You should also include all of your **_taxable investment accounts_** including bank accounts, GICs CDs, stocks, bonds, mutual funds, segregated funds and any investment outside your tax-deferred retirement accounts. These accounts are taxable, since they earn income or capital gains on an annual basis. An exception to this is a mutual fund set up in a Capital or Corporate Class structure. Such funds can defer income for many years. When you take or receive income from the fund, it generally receives preferential tax treatment as a capital gain. For purposes of this worksheet you should include any Corporate Class mutual funds under taxable investment accounts.

It's important to list only assets that can provide income. Your home or vacation property, for instance, should not be listed here unless you are renting them out to provide a source of income.

Important Note for Step 1 & 2: Make sure to fill in the subtotal sections. You'll use them later when completing the Retirement Spending Funnel.

Step 3: Determine Your Income Gap & Lump Sum Needs

Now it's time to take the information from the first two worksheets and transfer the subtotals to the **Retirement Spending Funnel.** This step will determine two things. First, you'll see if you have a shortfall or gap in your income relative to your expenses. If there's a gap, you'll see how much it is. You can then try to fill it by generating income from your available assets. Second, you'll see how much you need to set aside as a lump sum or reserve out of your available assets for an esteem or legacy expense. You may end up with some conflicting goals at this point, and that's ok. It's better to determine that now and sort it out before you start spending your money. In the next step you'll further prioritize your goals when selecting products.

> **It's important to list only assets that can provide income. Your home or vacation property, for instance, should not be listed here unless you are renting them out to provide a source of income.**

Below are the steps to determine your Income Gap & Lump Sum needs:

1. Transfer your Guaranteed Income subtotal from the Income/Expense Worksheet to the Guaranteed

Income box in the top left corner of the Funnel worksheet. Put this same number into the Guaranteed Income box on the right side of the funnel in the Gap Calculator section.

2. Transfer your expense category subtotals (Basic, What-if, Social, Esteem and Legacy Expenses) to the corresponding boxes in the funnel.

3. Add up the amounts in the first 3 expense categories (Basic, What if, and Social) and transfer that total to the Expenses box found in the Gap Calculator section of the Funnel (right side).

4. Calculate your Gap. In the Gap Calculator section, subtract your expense number from your Guaranteed Income. Now place that number in the Income Gap box. If this is a positive number, you can cover all your expenses with your guaranteed income. If it's a negative number, you'll need to find a way to generate that income.

5. Add your Esteem Expense number to your Legacy Expense number and place the total in the Lump Sum Needs box under the heading Funding Matrix at the bottom right of the funnel.

Congratulations. You've just determined the two critical numbers you need for your Retirement Income Plan.

Step 4: Determine your Product Allocation

Now you know how much income you need to fill your Income gap and how much to set aside for your Esteem and Legacy expenses. The next step is to figure out how to fund them. In this step you'll combine elements of product allocation theory with my Funding Matrix worksheet. This will help you decide which products to use and in what proportions to achieve your goals.

To do this you need the Funding Matrix Worksheet, your completed Available Assets Worksheet, and your completed Retirement Spending Funnel. For each account in your Funding Matrix you have to select the type of product or combination of products (GLIB, Annuity, SWP, Other) you want to use for each of the investments you currently own (retirement and taxable investment accounts). If this sounds complicated, don't worry. I'll show you how to do it. It's actually quite simple.

The products you select will depend on a number of factors. You may find that you have to re-prioritize your overall goals a couple of times and possibly make some concessions. Remember to consider the specific risks you think apply most to your situation. Is it inflation, sequence of returns, the cost of future healthcare or longevity that you're most concerned about? Also, applying the goal achievement attributes (Access, Emotion, Estate Wishes and Fees) will be helpful when deciding how to allocate your money among the different products.

The hardest thing for most people to figure out is if they have enough assets to address both their income needs and their esteem and legacy goals. After all you can't have your cake and eat it too. With this process, you can figure all that out in bite-sized chunks.

Your specific priorities will determine the area you address first. If your focus is on ensuring that you have an income throughout retirement then start there. Work on positioning assets to generate your needed income. If your esteem and legacy goals are more important, then you should address them first. I will address lump sum needs for esteem and legacy expenses first, for no other reason than that's how I do it with my private consulting clients.

> Bill & Jane have limited available assets: $100,000 of savings in a taxable investment account. They need to generate an additional $5000 to cover expenses, but at the same time want to ensure that they can leave that money for their disabled child. If they set aside all that money for their child they won't be able to generate the needed income. If on the other hand they invest to generate income for themselves, there may be nothing left for their child. In this case Bill & Jane will need to seriously consider which goal is most important and pick the products accordingly.

How to position your assets to fund Esteem and Legacy Expenses

Depending on your personal situation you may or may not need to fund esteem and legacy expenses. If you do, you should allocate assets to these expenses first, before allocating assets to creating your retirement income. The reason is simple. Esteem and Legacy expenses can require large lump sums. It's easier to set them aside first. Then you can see what's left to generate an income. If there isn't enough available for income generation, then you can pare down your esteem and legacy expenses. Let's get to it.

Funding your Esteem expenses

Typical esteem expenses include recreational vehicles or property, exclusive club memberships (golf or yacht), household renovation projects, or major travel plans costing 10s of thousands of dollars. You may need this money just before or very shortly after retirement. Therefore it's important to ensure that the money you set aside is secure and not subject to losses in the markets. It's also important to note that the 3 product categories from the Product Allocation model (SWP, Annuity and GLIB) don't apply to this type of expense, as they generally require lump sums, not an ongoing stream of income. This is why I've included a product category called Esteem in the Funding Matrix.

You first need to transfer the subtotaled amounts from your Available Assets worksheet to the Available Assets section at the top of the Funding Matrix. Remember to keep your retirement accounts separate from your taxable investment accounts. This is particularly important for tax reasons when selecting assets to fund your esteem expenses. If you have life insurance and real estate, including your home, transfer those numbers as well. Now look at your Retirement Spending Funnel. Transfer the Income Gap number, the esteem expense number and the legacy expense number to their corresponding boxes in the top right corner of the Funding Matrix.

It's now time to select assets to fund your esteem expenses. There are two key considerations when making this selection.

1. You will most likely use assets from your taxable investment accounts. For the most part, you have already paid taxes on these assets and won't be hit with a huge tax bill when you cash them out to make a large purchase like an RV, for example. Remember, most retirement accounts are tax deferred, which means you pay heavy taxes when you cash them out. It's far more efficient to use your tax-deferred assets to generate a stream of income and pay taxes a little bit at a time.

2. If you intend to pay for an esteem expense in the near term (1-3 years), the product you choose to set this money aside should be very secure. For instance, if you'll need $50,000 in 2 years to pay for a timeshare, you don't want to expose it to the risk of a 30% decline in the stock market, which would leave only $35,000 when you need the money.

Action Step
Take a look at your available assets in the Taxable Investment Accounts section at the top of the Funding Matrix. Now you need to decide what account or accounts to use for

your esteem expenses and set aside all or a portion of those accounts. Do this by picking a specific dollar amount from your chosen accounts and put it into the Esteem product category in the product options section.

You may have enough in one type of account to cover the whole expense, or you may have to take money from a number of accounts. Once you've done this, add up the amounts you've set aside to the Esteem product category row and transfer that total to the Total Esteem Expense Funding box on the far right side of the Funding Matrix under Product Options. This number should equal your Esteem Expenses number transferred from your Retirement Spending Funnel.

Mini Case Study: The soon to retire golf fanatics
Cecil and Margaret will be retiring in 4 years at age 60. They have been married for 35 years but never had any children. Margaret is a teacher and Cecil is a police officer. Because of their chosen careers they will have very good defined benefit pensions. They're both fanatics about golf, but have never had time to play as much as they'd like. When they retire, they want to join an exclusive golf club near their home so they can devote more time to their passion.

To join the club they'll need $75,000 in two years, when they retire. In addition they'll need to pay annual dues of $5,000. Between the two of them they have taxable investment accounts as follows: $25,000 in cash, $50,000 in bonds, $35,000 in GICs, and a long-term balanced mutual fund portfolio worth $140,000. With such a range of accounts they have a number of options available to pay for the golf membership and the annual dues.

Chapter 13: Mixing psychology with math to create your retirement income plan 219

They also want to set aside cash for emergencies or opportunities. Although they are healthy now, they are concerned about the possibility of long-term health care costs.

Taking all this into consideration Cecil and Margaret decide on the following product allocation to fund their esteem expense. They will allocate the $35,000 in GICs and $40,000 in bonds for the purpose of funding the golf membership. They won't risk using mutual funds in case of a market correction in the next four years. They'll now have $25,000 in a cash reserve, $10,000 in bonds, and $140,000 in mutual funds for other goals.

Even though they feel their pension income should be adequate to cover the full cost of the annual membership dues, they never want to come up short. Margaret did her research and found a GLIB that can provide this income. It will give them a 5% bonus for each of the 4 years before they retire. When they retire, the GLIB will provide a 4% guaranteed income for life starting at age 60.

They decide to purchase the GLIB now with $90,000 from their mutual fund account. By the time they retire, they will have accumulated 4 years of bonuses, which means the GLIB's guaranteed income base will be up to $126,000 ($90,000 + $36,000 bonus). Based on $126,000 the GLIB will pay $5,040 per year ($126,000 X 4%). Once their OAS and CPP payments kick in at age 65, they will no longer need the income from the GLIB. When that happens they can choose to stop the GLIB payment or keep it going and find something else to spend the money on. They really like that flexibility.

After all is said and done, Cecil and Margaret will have the money set aside for the golf membership. They will have a guaranteed income stream to pay for the annual dues, and they will still have an emergency fund of $35,000 and $60,000 left in mutual funds.

Funding your Legacy Expenses

At this point, you should have transferred your available assets including life insurance and real estate to the Available Assets section of the Funding Matrix. As well you should have a number in the top right corner of the Funding Matrix in the Legacy Expense box. Now it's time to determine how to fund your Legacy Expenses.

Legacy expenses are not as simple to fund as other expense categories. For one thing, you need to determine if you want your legacy to be funded while you are alive or upon your death. I know talking about death is depressing. Most folks don't even want to think about it. But this distinction is critical, as it directly affects the choices you'll make to fund your legacy.

A legacy gift can be something more than a lump sum of money or a piece of property. In some cases, it may provide an ongoing source of income for a loved one. Most people fund their legacy expenses upon death, so let's get started and look at how you might do the same.

Funding Legacy Expenses upon Death:
Many people have a simple approach to funding their legacy upon death. It can be summed up in this statement: "Whatever's left after I'm gone will be my legacy". Another common approach is to designate certain property or

assets without setting a number to it. And finally, some choose to leave a specific dollar amount or apply their legacy gift to a specific purpose. In any case, if you want to leave something other than whatever's left, then you'll need a plan to ensure that it's there upon your death.

To fund your legacy expenses upon death, you can get the money from 3 sources: life insurance, real estate and investments (both retirement and taxable accounts). Each has its own pros and cons, but all 3 can be very effective. Let's look at how each option can work for you.

> For one thing, you need to determine if you want your legacy to be funded while you are alive or upon your death.

Life insurance is perhaps the easiest and most efficient way to fund your legacy. For clarification I am referring to permanent life insurance, not term insurance, since term insurance (with the exception of Term-100 coverage) will expire at some point and may not be available when you die.

Once insurance is in place, the money is paid out very quickly and directly to the beneficiary upon the insured persons' death. Quite often it's done within a few weeks, and in most cases the death benefit is completely tax-free.

If you have a life insurance policy in place and you're making premium payments, then there isn't much work to be done. This expense should already be accounted for in your what-if expenses section, and the policy value should be listed under Life Insurance in the Available Assets section of the Funding Matrix.

On the other hand, if you are contemplating new permanent life insurance, then you have two options. Once you know the new premium, you can pay it from your income – in which case you should add the insurance premium to your what-if expenses.

The other option is to use a dump-in feature offered on some insurance policies. Think of it as a one-time premium payment. You take a lump sum of money and dump it into the policy. The money is invested within the policy to cover the annual premium payments automatically. If it's set up correctly you shouldn't have to add money to this policy. In general, dump-ins involve universal life and some whole life contracts. To be any more specific about the details of such policies is well beyond the scope of this book.

To use the dump-in feature, decide how much money you want to set aside and then see how much insurance you can buy with that amount. Alternatively, you can decide how much insurance coverage you want, and that will tell you how much you'll need to dump in to make it happen.

Action Step
If you have existing insurance in place with no plans to add coverage, then you only have a few things to do. First, if your policy is not paid up and you are making premium payments, make sure they are listed in your what-if expenses. Then you need to allocate the insurance death benefit amount of your insurance policy or policies to the Legacy Funding section of the Funding Matrix in the insurance box. Next compare that number with your legacy expense and see if it meets the need. If not, then you can look to your other

assets (investments or real estate) to see if they can make up the difference, or buy more insurance. Whichever you decide to use, enter the number in the appropriate box in the Legacy Funding section of the Funding Matrix.

If you are considering new life insurance and plan to pay the premiums on a monthly or annual basis, follow the steps outlined above for existing insurance. You'll just have to wait to get the exact premium expense once your new life insurance is approved and in force.

If you are considering new coverage and want to use the dump-in feature, you have to take an additional step. Once you know the death benefit and how much you need for the dump-in, you'll have to figure out where you'll get the money. First assign the death benefit amount of this new policy to the Insurance box in the Legacy Funding section. Then decide which asset you want to use for the dump-in. Once done, you'll need to take that amount of money off the table by entering the amount in the Legacy box in the product option section for the asset you wish to use.

Using Insurance to Provide an Income for a Beneficiary
In some circumstances there is a need to provide an ongoing income to a beneficiary rather than giving a lump sum. Insurance can be used as the funding mechanism for this purpose. You will still follow the steps outlined above to ensure the legacy gift is accounted for. The only difference is how the insurance proceeds are paid out. Some insurance policies allow for an "annuity" to be created upon death for a specific beneficiary. For policies that don't have this type of settlement option, an alternative is to set up a testamentary

trust through a will. That trust would receive the proceeds of the insurance policy and then subsequently pay out an income to the person of your choosing, either using an annuity or some other strategy. If this is something you are considering, it's highly recommended that you seek advice from a professional insurance advisor and also get legal advice.

Mini Case Study: A recent widow takes care of her kids
Mary Beth retired 2 years ago with her husband Sam. Unfortunately, her situation changed drastically 3 months ago when Sam died of cancer. As a result, Mary Beth is in the process of trying to figure out her financial situation, and is working on her retirement income plan. Having just suffered the loss of her husband, the topic of estate planning is also on her mind. She's decided that she wants to ensure a legacy for each of her 3 children.

Two of her children have careers as professionals and make a very good income. Her youngest is an artist and has never been too interested in money. Mary Beth wants to be fair in what she leaves her children. She also feels the gifts don't have to be of equal monetary value in order to be fair, since her children are all so different.

Mary Beth has a home, a cottage, and a sizable investment portfolio, in part from the insurance proceeds she received when Sam died. She also has her own $200,000 permanent life insurance policy. Her son is the only child living in the same province. Aside from living out of province, neither of the girls has ever shown interest in the cottage. Her son loves the cottage and in fact has been looking after it for years.

Here's what Mary Beth has decided to do. She worries about her artist daughter and her ability to handle money. She is always giving her money here and there as it is. She feels the best thing she can do for her is to provide her with a stable ongoing income when she's gone. To do this she will select the annuity settlement option on the life insurance policy. So instead of $200,000, this daughter will get an income for life.

As for the cottage, she wants to give it to her son now. She knows this will trigger a capital gain and is willing to pay the capital gains tax out of her investments. To keep things fair, she also plans to give her two daughters a cash gift now, equivalent to the capital gains tax she will have to pay on the cottage.

Her other daughter will receive the proceeds from the sale of the family home. In the event that Mary Beth sells her home before she dies, she will assign a specific asset or dollar amount as a direct bequest to her eldest daughter. Any money left over from her investments will go to her estate and be divided equally among the 3 children.

Now she can move on and allocate her investments to generate her retirement income.

Real Estate holdings are another method of funding your legacy expense. Quite often clients say that they plan to spend all their money and just leave the house to the kids. That will be their legacy. This is a straightforward approach and very tax efficient, as well, since a principle residence is usually tax exempt (in Canada anyway).

There are two ways you can leave your home to someone. You can make a direct bequest in your will to a specified beneficiary or beneficiaries. They will then be free to do whatever they wish with the property. Or you can direct in your will that the house be sold with the proceeds going to the beneficiaries.

If you decide to sell the house and distribute the proceeds to your heirs, it may take some time to sell and transfer the money. As a funding strategy for your legacy expense, you should keep in mind that real estate values fluctuate, sometimes drastically, as recent events in the US have shown.

What about other real estate like recreational property, second homes or commercial property? They too can be left through your will in the same way as your principle residence. However, unlike your home, they'll be taxed. A few other issues also need your attention.

> Quite often clients say that they plan to spend all their money and just leave the house to the kids. That will be their legacy

No matter how you give this property, it will attract taxation upon your death. Taxes are usually assessed at time of death and must be paid within a specified period. If the taxes are due before the property can be sold, then a problem may arise, whether you choose to sell the asset or give it in kind.

If you leave the property in kind your heirs receive it directly, but they may not receive cash from the estate to pay the taxes. If they don't have enough money of their own to pay the taxes, they may have to sell the property just to pay them. Therefore if you're considering this option, you should ensure that funds are available to pay the tax man.

When it comes to real estate other than your home, you'll need to consider other factors as well. Do your intended beneficiaries even want the property? Not everyone wants to be a landlord, for example, so this could be an issue if you own commercial or rental property. Many people would prefer to have the money. If they do want the property, they may not be able to afford the ongoing property taxes and maintenance costs. Once again, you should discuss this with your intended heirs before you assign the property as the funding mechanism for your legacy expense.

Action Step

If this is a strategy you plan to use, then all you have to do is allocate the value of your home, cottage or commercial prop-erty to the Legacy funding section of the Funding Matrix and see if that's enough to cover your Legacy Expense. If not then you will have to look at other sources as well. If the property you wish to give is likely to attract taxation, you may also want to assign some other investment asset to pay the tax man. To do this, select an investment from your available assets and allocate a dollar figure to the legacy box in the product options section. How you leave your home to your heirs is certainly something you should discuss with them before you make the designation in your will.

Mini Case Study: The Retired Business Owners
Bill and Nancy are retired business owners. They recently sold their company for a significant sum and kept the commercial property, worth $2 million. They lease it back

to the new owners and use the income to supplement their retirement. They have one son (Roger) and 2 grandchildren. Like many people they plan to spend their money in retirement and leave whatever's left to their son. They especially want to pass on the commercial property. They see this as an opportunity to leave a legacy from their hard work for the next two or more generations. To do this they have set up a testamentary trust in their wills. The property will go into the trust upon their death, along with some additional money to cover future maintenance expenses. Roger will be the income beneficiary, meaning he'll be paid all the income that the property generates during his lifetime. The property itself will never go to him, but instead will go equally to the two grandchildren upon Rogers' death. Bill and Nancy discussed this with Roger and he is on board with the idea. No matter how much they joke about it, he knows that mom and dad will not likely spend all their money, no matter how hard they try.

Investments are the third source of funding for a legacy expense. The strategy can be as simple as leaving your heirs whatever you don't use during your lifetime. This is how many people address their legacy wishes.

However, if you have a specific legacy goal and want to fund it using some of your investments, then you have to allocate them for that purpose. You'll want to determine which ones to leave and how best to leave them. As with recreational or commercial properties, you should consider taxation and timing and how you want your heir to receive the money.

An investment gift may be reduced by taxation, for example. Capital gains and estate taxes (where applicable) can have a considerable effect on the amount of money transferred at death. You should also keep in mind that, even if you give an investment in-kind, taxes may still apply, which the estate must pay.

Taxation on retirement accounts (RRSPs, RRIFs, LIFs, LIRAs, 401(k)'s etc.) is perhaps the most significant area of concern. Remember, these accounts are tax deferred and will be heavily taxed upon death, with a few exceptions. In Canada, retirement accounts transferred to anyone other than a surviving spouse or dependent child are taxed as income in the year of death. This can easily put one into the top marginal tax bracket of 40% or higher in the year of death. To be prepared, you should make funds available in the estate to pay these taxes.

Estates can and do take considerable time to settle. If your situation is fairly straightforward, this won't be an issue. If your estate is complex, timing can complicate things when it comes to the transfer of assets. Taxes are assessed at time of death, for example, and must be paid within a specified period. A complex estate can delay the transfer of assets to your heirs. If this is a concern, you can select products to make the transfer quick and efficient.

For instance, you could put certain investments in joint name with right of survivorship. This strategy comes with a bunch of downsides, the most serious of which is giving up partial control of the asset. If you're considering joint ownership, you should do so only after serious consideration.

Using a Segregated fund is a much better option. With a segregated fund you can name a direct beneficiary and still retain full control of the asset. Upon death the account is paid out directly to the beneficiary outside of the estate. Keep in mind that, even though this money can bypass the estate, taxes may still apply. This is especially true if you use this product for your tax-deferred retirement accounts. You should make provisions in the estate to pay any taxes that might arise from this transfer.

Another option is to use a Tax Free Savings Account (TFSA) in Canada. In most provinces and territories you can list a successor owner or named beneficiary. By doing so, you can pass on your TFSA outside of your estate. However, unlike other retirement accounts or taxable investment accounts, this transfer in most cases doesn't attract taxation when it goes to a beneficiary. The rules are a bit complex, and they vary slightly from province to province. Set up properly, a TFSA can be transferred quickly and tax-free. You can learn more about TFSAs at the Canada Revenue Agency website: www.cra.gc.ca.

Finally, before selecting any assets for your legacy expense, figure out how you want your heir to receive the money. For most people this is very straightforward. The asset will be either given in kind or sold for cash which is then distributed through the will. But some situations may require a different strategy.

For instance, an intended heir might require ongoing care because of a physical or mental disability. Or the heir may be a spendthrift who can't handle finances. In either case, receiving a lump sum of money or an investment in-kind may not be appropriate. A better option may be to provide a lifetime income. To achieve this, you might consider setting up a testamentary trust or specify the purchase of a life annuity for your beneficiary in your will.

Action Step:
If you want to leave a legacy using a specific investment asset, then you have to decide how much to give and what asset to use. In the Funding Matrix worksheet select an account or accounts from your available assets and allocate them to the Legacy funding box in the product options section. If the asset is likely to attract taxation, you may also assign an additional investment asset to pay the tax man. Select an investment from your available assets and allocate a dollar figure to the legacy box in the product options section. If you've selected several investment accounts to fund your legacy, add them up and put the total in the box for Investments in the Legacy Funding section of the Funding Matrix.

If you have a complex situation or significant assets, I recommended strongly that you seek professional financial and legal advice to set up your legacy plan.

Mini Case Study: The Second Marriage (go round)
Tom and Marsha are happily married, each for the second time. Tom has 2 boys from his first marriage, and Marsha has 3 girls, but they have no children together. They're about 6 years from retirement and want to get a plan in place now. As part of that plan they are trying to decide what to do with the money they each brought to their second marriage.

Neither of them has a pension from work. Tom has always been a saver, and he has managed to amass a nice sum in his tax-deferred retirement accounts. A few years ago he also inherited $80,000 when his parents died. As part of Marsha's divorce from her first husband she received $50,000 in tax-deferred retirement funds (RRSP). She has also saved $15,000 in her Tax Free Savings Account and plans to keep building it.

They've agreed to list each other as beneficiaries on their tax-deferred retirement accounts. This way they can avoid paying a bunch of taxes when the first of them dies, and it will provide an ongoing income for the survivor. Their dilemma is how to address their other investments from their previous marriages. Tom wants his money to go to his kids and Marsha's to hers. Assets they build together they'll deal with through their will and divide equally among all 5 children.

Tom wants his boys to get the $80,000 he inherited plus whatever it accumulates before he dies. He decides to buy a segregated fund with a 100% death benefit guarantee. The contract allows him to list his two boys as direct beneficiaries, which will allow the money to pass outside of his estate. He can access the money if and when he needs it, and the original $80,000 will be protected with the 100% guarantee. Tom is aware that, even though this money will pass outside the estate, it will likely attract capital gains tax in the future. To address this Tom lists his estate as a 20% beneficiary on the segregated fund. This ensures that money will flow into the estate to cover the tax bill on the capital gain.

Marsha wants her girls to receive the proceeds from her Tax Free Savings Account upon her passing. Instead of listing Tom as successor owner, and because they live in Ontario, she lists her girls as beneficiaries on this account. This way they can receive the money directly and tax-free. She doesn't like investing in the markets, so she invests the money in guaranteed investment certificates inside her tax free savings account. This way the capital is protected and she doesn't pay tax on the interest. If she needs the money she can get it, depending on the maturity dates of the GICs.

Funding Legacy Expenses while alive:

Rather than waiting until death, some people prefer to provide their legacy gift while they're still alive. This way they can experience the joy that comes from giving. If this makes sense for you and the gift involves your assets or income, then you should account for it at this step. Generally this type of legacy gift can be cash, an investment account or a real estate asset.

Much like funding an esteem expense, you should keep in mind that any money allocated for this purpose will no longer be available to create extra income for you. For example, a common living-legacy gift is money that enables an adult child to buy a home. Once you've given that money and the home is purchased, it's difficult to get it back.

Another consideration is taxes. If you plan to give a large gift, then you need to consider the applicable taxes. An exception is a gift to charity, which might get a tax break. If you have an investment portfolio worth $100,000 that you want to give to your daughter, for example, you should determine the applicable capital gain and give your daughter the net amount, after tax. Otherwise, you'll have to take money from somewhere else to pay the tax man, and this could affect some of your other goals.

Action Step
Once you've decided how much to give as your living legacy, you need to decide where that gift will come from. Take a look at your available assets and real estate in your Funding Matrix worksheet and select the asset you wish to use. Now transfer the dollar figure that you wish to give and place it in either the Investment or Real Estate box of the Legacy Funding section of the Funding Matrix (depending on what you are giving).

> Rather than waiting until death, some people prefer to provide their legacy gift while they're still alive. This way they can experience the joy that comes from giving.

If you plan to give real estate then you'll likely transfer the whole amount associated with a particular property, since you generally don't give just a portion of real estate.

On the other hand, when gifting money from an investment, you could give only a portion if you wish. But be careful. This could lead to double dipping. If you are using an investment asset for a legacy gift, make sure that you also transfer the amount of the gift and place it in the box farther down the column in the Legacy row of the Product Options section.

Mini Case Study: Parents helping out their daughter

Ed and Joanna have $100,000 in a taxable GIC investment portfolio. Their daughter Tracy just gave birth to twins and the grandparents are thrilled. With two older siblings their daughter's family has outgrown their small car and is in need of a minivan. Unfortunately their son-in-law has been laid off at the quarry, and they can't afford to buy one. Ed and Joanna want to ensure that their grandchildren are safe when on the road, so they decide to give Tracy $35,000 from their GIC portfolio for the minivan.

Capital gains tax won't be an issue when using a GIC to fund this gift, since GICs earn annual taxable interest. By providing this living legacy gift to Tracy they know they have taken $35,000 off the table for other uses. This leaves them with only $65,000 in their GIC portfolio to help fund their income goal.

Position your assets to fund an Income Gap

Now that you've set aside assets for your esteem and legacy expenses, it's time to work on the income part of your plan. Here you will determine if your remaining available assets can generate an adequate amount to cover your income gap. You'll also decide how much of that income, if any, you want to be guaranteed. You'll do this by allocating your available assets to the 3 product types discussed earlier – a guaranteed living income benefit (GLIB), an annuity or a systematic withdrawal plan (SWP).

People working with financial advisors can get assistance from them. If you don't have an advisor, you'll have to do some calculations on your own. I'll show you how. You'll need these calculations for each of the 3 product options.

In the next section, you'll find out how to estimate the income from each of the 3 product categories. Then I'll outline the specific steps you need to take to create your customized product allocation using my worksheets.

Calculating Income for the 3 Product Categories
Even if you're working with a financial advisor, it's a good idea to know how income is determined for a GLIB, an annuity or a SWP. Having a clear understanding of how each one works will ultimately help relieve fear in the future when the markets go down. What follows is a brief explanation of how you can do just that.

GLIB: GLIB income payments are based on a simple percentage calculation, typically 5% of the amount deposited into the plan. Most plans require the plan-holder to be at least 65 years old before they start providing this 5% income for life. For the years when you don't withdraw any income, you may receive a bonus. These bonuses can increase your future payments. Other plans base payments on a lower percentage if you want to take a lifetime income before age 65. And some have options to increase the guaranteed percentage income if you wait until after age 65 to take the income.

Most plans also have a reset feature. The insurance company will periodically compare the actual market value with the contract's guaranteed value. If the market value has increased above the guaranteed value, then the company may raise the contract's guaranteed value. This will increase the future guaranteed income. For our purposes, let's simply assume you get a 5% payment on the capital you allocate to a GLIB.

If you know how much income you need, simply divide that number by 5%. For example: If you need $10,000, then divide $10,000 by 5% to find that you'll need to allocate $200,000 to the GLIB.

On the other hand, if you want to allocate a set amount of money to a GLIB, then simply multiply that number by 5% to determine how much income it will produce.

For example: If you allocate $50,000, then you can assume an income of $2,500 a year.

For a more precise estimate based on your age or the features of a specific GLIB product, you'll need a projection or illustration. An advisor can help. Not working with an advisor? You may get an illustration from the website of a GLIB supplier in your province or state. Some companies provide online GLIB calculators.

People often ask whether they should use tax-deferred retirement accounts (RRSPs, RRIFs, IRAs, 401Ks) or taxable investment accounts for a GLIB. While there is no right or wrong answer, I prefer to use retirement accounts. Here's why.

Many people don't have a workplace pension. These people generally contribute to a retirement account as a way to save for their retirement. These retirement accounts replace the pension they don't have and should be treated like a pension. This is where the GLIB fits well. One of the main features of a GLIB is to provide a lifetime income, much like a pension plan. No matter how the markets perform, a GLIB provides a minimum income for life, with the added benefit of potential increases in income through resets in positive markets.

You can regard a GLIB as your own personal pension plan, but only if you treat it that way. That means, once you allocate a certain amount of your resources to the GLIB to produce a specified income, you shouldn't touch that money for any other purpose. After all, if you had a pension plan you wouldn't go to the pension administrator and request a lump sum of cash to buy a new car.

> If you used retirement accounts for other purposes such as large lump-sum purchases you'd need significantly more money to account for the taxes.

Another reason to use retirement accounts for a GLIB is taxation. Retirement accounts are tax deferred, meaning that you have no choice but to pay taxes when you access them. But even though every dollar that comes out of a retirement account is taxed as income, you pay the tax a little bit at a time if you use them for an income stream over a long period. Meanwhile, the bulk of the account continues to grow tax-deferred. If you used retirement accounts for other purposes such as large lump-sum purchases you'd need significantly more money to account for the taxes.

Action Step
Take a look at your Available Assets and decide how much if any you want to allocate to a GLIB. Be mindful of any

portion you may already have allocated to other goals. When you've decided on how much to allocate to a GLIB, enter that amount under GLIB in the Product Options section for your retirement accounts and your investment accounts, whichever you decide to use. Remember to enter the amount of income it will generate in the income section at the bottom of the worksheet. This number will be based on your calculation or an illustration from your advisor

CANADIAN CASE STUDY

In Canada, when using your retirement accounts inside the GLIB you'll get an added benefit of receiving the government's prescribed minimum income or the GLIB guaranteed minimum whichever is higher. If markets perform well you'll likely get a higher income than the minimum 5%. If markets perform poorly, you are at least assured of the 5% income based on the amount you originally invested in the plan.

Here's how it works: The annual RRIF minimum income is calculated by using a prescribed percentage multiplied by the account balance at the end of the year. Starting at age 71, this percentage is 7.38% and it increases each year. If the markets perform better than the prescribed RRIF percentage then your income will increase because your pot of money is still growing. In the event of a prolonged market downturn, while the required withdrawal percentage goes up, the account balance shrinks. This could eventually lead to a lower income. With a GLIB, once this calculation leads to an income that's lower than the 5% guaranteed income, the plan starts paying the 5% amount, based on your deposits to the GLIB.

Life Annuity: Unlike the GLIB there is no simple calculation that applies equally to everyone when estimating income from a Life Annuity. The calculation is based on a number of factors, including: your age, sex, life expectancy and current interest rates, among other things. Because of this, you'll need a personalized annuity quote to determine the assets you'll need for a specified lifetime income. A life insurance agent can provide a quote. Alternatively, just Google "life annuity quote" and go to one of the websites such as www.immediateannuities.com.

Whether you ask your life insurance agent or use an online resource for a quote, you can approach it in one of two ways. You could say – I need x amount of income from an annuity, so how much money do I have to deposit to get it? Or you could say – I have x amount of money to put into an annuity, so how much income will that provide? Depending on how much income you want to guarantee and the other assets you have to allocate to other products, you may have to play with the annuity numbers.

When getting an annuity quote, keep in mind the guaranteed period. With a life annuity with a guaranteed period, the insurance company guarantees to make income payments for a minimum period. This ensures that you get most, if not all, of your capital back if you die before your annuity payments equaled the amount you've paid for the annuity. Without such a guarantee, you could deposit x amount of money expecting a payment for life and receive only 2 payments if you die within 2 months.

Whenever possible, you should choose a guarantee period that ensures payments equal to your deposit to the annuity. If you die before all payments are received, then the remaining payments can continue or be paid out as a lump sum to a designated beneficiary. Naturally, there is a cost to this option in the form of a larger deposit for the same amount of income.

On the other hand, if you need to maximize your income and aren't concerned with leaving a legacy, then opting for no guarantee on the annuity may be the way to go.

Action Step
Once you have the annuity quote, enter the amount of assets you'll use for the annuity under Annuity in the Product Options Section. Be mindful of any portion you may already have allocated to other goals. You should also enter the amount of income the annuity will produce in the corresponding income section in the column at the bottom of the matrix, under Income Options.

Mini Case Study: Annuity for sure, but in whose name?
Al and Betty are both 65 and are contemplating retirement this year. They've completed their Retirement Spending Funnel and have determined that they will have a $6,000 annual income gap.

They live a modest lifestyle with no major travel plans or expenses planned. They own their home outright and have a total of $150,000 saved for their future. Their biggest concern is how to cover their income shortfall, even though they'd like to leave money to their kids or to charity. They also have no tolerance for risk in the markets, which is why most of their savings are in bank accounts and GICs. They also think that financial companies charge far too much in fees, so they will not consider purchasing a GLIB for their needed income.

Consequently when looking at their options they've decided on a traditional life annuity with a guarantee period. This way they believe they can have their income guaranteed for as long as they live. If they die young, there will be something for the kids and the United Way. The only thing they aren't sure about is who should buy the annuity. Should it be Al or Betty or should they buy it jointly, as Betty's sister suggested? For help they ask their insurance advisor for some quotes. This is what he provides:

For a lifetime income of $6,000 annually, with a 20-year guarantee period:

- In his name, Al would have to deposit approximately $98,934.
- In her name, Betty would have to deposit approximately $102,500
- Purchased jointly, they would have to deposit approximately $107,916

Al and Betty were surprised at the difference in the amounts they'd have to deposit to get $6,000 in annual income. They were especially surprised by the joint number. While it would cost them less to buy the annuity in Al's name, Betty's income could be at risk after 20 years if Al died first. His income will be in jeopardy after 20 years if Betty buys the annuity and dies before Al. The joint annuity option is the most expensive. What it offers, though, is a guarantee of the $6,000 annual income for life, no matter who dies first. And

Chapter 13: Mixing psychology with math to create your retirement income plan 243

if they both die before 85, there will be something left for the kids because of the guarantee.

Even though it will cost the most in terms of how much they have to deposit, Al and Betty decide on the joint life annuity. They don't ever want to worry about income, and they feel this is the best way to accomplish that. As it turns out Betty's younger sister does know a thing or two.

Managed Money with a Systematic Withdrawal Plan (SWP):

Recall that SWP stands for **s**ystematic **w**ithdrawal **p**lan. In other words, this is a plan that allows you regularly (systematically) to take out a set amount of money from an investment that you own. A SWP is typically associated with a mutual fund account. However it can be used with any investment that allows access to the capital for periodic withdrawals including: a mutual fund, segregated fund, stock or bond portfolio, ETF portfolio, GIC or CD portfolio.

A SWP is more flexible than a GLIB or an annuity, because you get to decide how much to take out and when to do it. You can also start and stop whenever you wish, and you have full access to the capital, at any time. However, unlike a GLIB or annuity, the income is not guaranteed, and the capital is subject to market and sequence of return risk.

Also, unlike a GLIB or annuity, a SWP doesn't allow you to determine a set income amount determined as a function of the product. You simply pick the amount you want to withdraw from the account. However, you do need to consider the rate at which you withdraw the money compared to the rate of return you earn on the investment. If you take out more on a percentage basis than the investment earns, you will deplete some of the capital with every withdrawal. If that continues, or if a major market correction occurs, you could eventually deplete the investment completely. Encroaching on your capital is a personal choice. Some people never want to touch their principle if they can avoid it, while others don't mind dipping into it. Still others have no choice.

To make your money last as long as possible, you should set a withdrawal rate that's lower than the expected return on the investment. Also, you should consider an investment vehicle that has an income component in addition to capital growth. Then you'll have a better chance of making your money last.

> **To make your money last as long as possible, you should set a withdrawal rate that's lower than the expected return on the investment**

The reason is simple. Let's say your account is only growth-based and you take out a 4% SWP. If the account has a negative year, you'll have to dip into your capital. On the other hand if there is negative growth, but the account still earns income of 4% from dividends and interest, then you won't have to touch the capital.

The actual amount of a SWP can be determined in a couple of ways. You can simply say I need X amount of money a year and start drawing that from a specified account, hoping it lasts as long as you need it. If you need $2,500 a year and have an account worth $50,000, simple math says this account could last for 20 years ($50,000/$2,500=20), not accounting for fees or a rate of return. In the real world, though, it's subject to risk and could lose value as markets fluctuate unless it's in a guaranteed investment like a bank account, GIC, or CD.

A better way of determining a SWP is to first make an assumption on your expected rate of return. Then pick a percentage or a dollar amount to withdraw as your SWP. If capital preservation is your goal, then this amount should be equal to or less than the return at your assumed rate.

You should also consider the impact of fees charged to manage the account. For example, if you expect the investment to earn income of 4.5% in addition to any growth, then you could withdraw as much as 4.5% without dipping into the capital. But if you pay a management fee of 2%, then your net earnings before the SWP will be only 2.5% (4.5% - 2%). If the plan doesn't earn at least 2% on top of its net income of 2.5%, you'll encroach on your capital.

An Example

> Let's say you have $100,000 in an investment account that you wish to allocate to your SWP. The investments in this account are a mix of income and growth. The account is expected to earn 4.5% in interest and dividend income (after fees). This means that the account will earn $4,500 annually. If you also set the SWP at 4.5%, you'll receive an income payment of $4,500. If however you need more income than that, and you set the initial SWP withdrawal rate at 6%, you'll take out $6,000 a year but earn only $4,500. Assuming no growth in the account in a given year, this would result in an encroachment on your principle of $1,500. For any year that the growth component is more than 1.5% you will not encroach on your principle. Remember, though, encroaching on capital is not necessarily a bad thing and is a personal choice that only you can make.

Action Step

Take a look at your Available Assets in the top row of the Funding Matrix and decide how much if any should be allocated to a SWP. Be mindful of any portion you may have already allocated to other goals. When you've decided on how much to allocate to a SWP, enter that amount under SWP in the Product Options section for your registered accounts and your investment accounts. Remember to enter the amount of income the SWP will generate in the corresponding income section, in the same column at the bottom of the Matrix, in the Income Options section.

Completing Your Funding Matrix: A Summary

Now that I've provided some guidance on calculating the income for each of the 3 product types, it's time to summarize how to fill out the Funding Matrix. Below is a summary of the specific steps you need to take. This is the last part of the process. You will now allocate your investments to the specific products needed to create your additional retirement income.

1. Transfer the subtotaled amounts from your Available Assets Worksheet to the corresponding sections in the top part of the Funding Matrix under Available Assets. Be sure to keep the amounts from your Retirement Accounts (RRSPs, RRIFs, LIRA's, TFSAs, 401Ks and IRAs) separate from your taxable investment accounts. You'll notice that there are separate sections for them in both worksheets.

Chapter 13: Mixing psychology with math to create your retirement income plan 247

2. Consider which of the 3 products (SWP, Annuity, GLIB) best suits your situation for both your registered and taxable investment accounts. Keep in mind the Risk Achievement Attributes and Goal Achievement Attributes.

3. Allocate your investment accounts to the product options you have selected in step 2. Once you've decided on the product categories that best suit your situation, you can determine how much to allocate from each investment account to each of the products. Enter that number in the appropriate box under Product Options section in the middle of the Funding Matrix worksheet. Do this for both your registered and taxable investment accounts.

4. Don't over-allocate. Make sure you haven't allocated more than you have available from each of the accounts in the available assets section. Remember, you may have allocated some or all of a certain account for an esteem or legacy expense. To double check yourself, add up the amounts you've allocated to each product category. Do this for each account, and put that total in the bottom of the column of the Product Options section. This total must equal the amount at the top of the column for each account listed in the available assets section.

5. Calculate the income for each one of the products that you've selected and entered in step 3.

6. Enter the income amount you calculated for each of the chosen products into the Income Options section of the worksheet. Depending on which products you're using, you'll enter these income amounts as Annuity, SWP or GLIB. This section is found directly below the Product Options section of the worksheet.

7. Determine your total guaranteed income. Do this by adding all the amounts for Annuities and GLIBs in their respective rows of the Income Options section. Now enter those numbers in the guaranteed column of the Total Incomes section in the bottom right corner of the worksheet. Then add the Annuity total to the GLIB total and enter it at the bottom of the Guaranteed Income column.

8. Determine your total non-guaranteed/variable income. Do this by adding up all the amounts entered for SWPs in the SWP row of the Income Options section. Enter that total in the Variable Income column of the Total Income section in the bottom right corner of the worksheet. Now enter that number at the bottom of the Variable Income column.

9. Determine the Total Income generated from your product allocation. Do this by adding the Guaranteed and Variable Income totals together and entering them in the Gross Income box at the bottom of the worksheet.

Chapter 13: Mixing psychology with math to create your retirement income plan 249

10. Enter your estimated income tax in the Tax box below the Gross income in the bottom right corner of the worksheet. Remember the old saying: "It's not what you earn that's important, it's what you get to keep". If you need help estimating you taxes, ask your advisor or go to www.fearlessretirementresources.com for additional resources.

11. Calculate your Net Income for your product allocation strategy. Do this by subtracting your estimated taxes from your Gross income. This is the bottom-line number that you'll have available to cover your Income Gap.

   Congratulations! You have now determined the amount of income your product allocation strategy can produce for you. If it's not sufficient to cover your income gap you'll have to go back and make some changes to the products selected or the amount of assets you've allocated to generating income. You may have to allocate less money to esteem and legacy expense, and more to your income-producing products.
   If you'd like to use an automated calculator to complete your Retirement Income Plan, please visit www.fearlessretirementresources.com. The Fearless Retirement Calculator incorporates all of the worksheets introduced in this book to automate much of this process.

Chapter 14: Bringing it all together

Some would say you can never get to the end of a rainbow, because there really is no actual end. Those same people would likely argue that the pot of gold is just as elusive as a leprechaun. So what was the point of this book if you can never find the mythical pot of gold at the end of the rainbow?

Well, when it comes to getting to retirement (the end of the rainbow) and using your pot of gold (retirement savings) both of these are truly attainable. To do so though, you must change your way of thinking and use some very basic time-tested and proven principles.

That was the overall purpose of this book. And I hope I delivered this by covering four main goals through the book.

The first was to put this concept of retirement into a whole new perspective. For those of you who are not yet retired but are facing it in the next 5 to 15 years, the time you spend in retirement could indeed be as long as the time you spent during your working years. You need to think about what you might be doing for those potential 30 years and how you're going to pay for the things you do. Such a long retirement isn't a certainty for everyone, but you need to ask yourself, What if it is for me? If, in fact, you do have such a long life ahead of you, you need to know about some new challenges and understand how they might affect your life.

Identifying these new challenges and making them real for you was the second goal of this book. When it comes to planning for the way you'll spend your retirement and, more to the point, how you'll pay for it, identifying the things that could cause you financial difficulties is of crucial importance. If you aren't aware of these risks or if you ignore their existence, you may never have a chance to avoid them or at least reduce their effect on your life. Longevity, sequence of returns and the cost of future health care may never have occurred to you before reading this book. After reading it, I hope you see how significantly these risks could change what you can do and enjoy during your golden years.

> You need to think about what you might be doing for those potential 30 years and how you're going to pay for the things you do. Such a long retirement isn't a certainty for everyone, but you need to ask yourself, What if it is for me?

Figuring out the things that could potentially derail your plans for retirement is only the first step to ensuring you can do all the things you want and deserve to do in this later stage of life. With that said, the third goal of the book was to help you create a plan to address these risks, either by eliminating them or at the very least reducing their impact. By using the worksheets and tools I've provided, you'll have the building blocks to determine just how much money you'll require to achieve all that you want in retirement. These tools will not only assist you in determining where your income will come from and what you'll be spending your money on, they'll also help you determine how much you might need to deal with the risks that could blow up your plans.

By combining these tools with the new concept of product allocation you'll be able to figure out the best way to use your financial assets (savings and investments) for your retirement. Determining how to fund your retirement without worry of running out of money is the key to the whole process. The old-school methods simply don't work anymore given the specific new risks facing the boomer generation. Once you do this, you can go about doing all the things that are important to you without financial worry.

In this book I have hopefully opened your eyes to the various risks you may face and have given you a way to create your own plan for the future. Many people still want to, or need to deal with a financial professional in some capacity to put their plans into action. Taking into account the potential financial advisor risks I've identified brings up a whole new problem. Namely, what should you look for in an advisor and how do you go about finding the right kind of advisor? This was the basis for the forth goal of the book.

In today's complex world, in an ever-changing financial landscape, you need to protect your money from unscrupulous scam artists or just plain ineffective advisors. In three chapters I went into considerable detail on how to check out potential advisors in an effort to reduce these risks. Furthermore I showed you a way to assess if an advisor is planning or transaction focused.

It is my sincere hope that you'll be able to take the information and strategies I've presented in this book and form the basis for your own retirement income plan. Learn some lessons from the examples and case studies so you can avoid the mistakes that others have made. At the very least, if you can gain a good understanding of what you need to do by using the tools I've given you, you'll be able to meet with any advisor and determine whether or not he can help you to achieve your retirement dream without worry. On the other hand, for the do-it-yourselfers, by using all the resources I've provided, you'll be able to create your own plan to implement in your own way.

> In today's complex world, in an ever-changing financial landscape, you need to protect your money from unscrupulous scam artists or just plain ineffective advisors.

So go ahead, use this information and the additional resources found at www.FearlessRetirementResources.com to take control of your future. Get off the treadmill. If you do, you'll indeed find you can reach and protect your very own pot of gold at the end of the rainbow.

To quote one of my father's favorite sayings - "He who hesitates, loses". So go ahead and do this now. The longer you hesitate to address this issue, the less likely you'll have a retirement without financial worry.

END

Appendix 1: Long Term Care Insurance and Retirement Income Insurance Explained

What exactly is long term care (LTC) insurance and how can it help? Recall back in chapter 3 I talked about the cost of future health care and how it could be one of the biggest risks you'll face in retirement. The specific risk is not being able to pay for a long-term health-care expense, especially one that could add upwards of $20,000 a year to your other expenses. If you have substantial savings set aside for such expenses then you have essentially self-insured.

LTC insurance is for people who have not self-insured. At its most basic level LTC insurance works like any other insurance. You pay a premium to an insurance company to cover a certain risk. In return the insurance company agrees to pay you money if you are affected by that risk. In the event that you require ongoing assistance for a long-term health need, a LTC insurance policy will help you cover those costs.

The amount of coverage depends on the amount of benefit you purchase, and the premium reflects the amount of coverage. Like other types of insurance, when you make a claim you have to prove that you qualify for the benefit. With all LTC insurance policies you have to meet certain definitions of care before the benefit is paid.

In general, to qualify for a benefit payment the insured must be unable to perform 2 or more activities of daily living or suffer from cognitive impairment. Activities of daily living are defined as: dressing, eating, bathing, toileting, transferring and continence.

> After being on claim for 1½ years she will have received all the money back that she paid out in premiums over the 20 years.

There are also many bells and whistles that can be added to a basic policy, and they vary from company to company. A description of all the options is beyond the scope of this book. But here's an example of how LTC insurance works.

Long Term Care Insurance In Action

Setting the stage:

Samantha is a single 55-year-old with a decent pension and some savings set aside for retirement at 65. Her total net worth including her home is approximately $450,000. Samantha is caring for her mother, who suffers from Alzheimer's, and she sees firsthand the effects of not having enough money set aside for care. Consequently she is concerned about the future cost of her own health care, and she doesn't want to be forced to sell her home like her mother. Based on her future pension income and savings she feels that an additional $1,500 per month of income from insurance would really help, in the event that she needed care.

The Solution:

Based on Samantha's age and the fact that she is currently in good health, she can buy a <u>basic</u> LTC Insurance policy from a leading Canadian insurance company.

Policy Features:

- Monthly premium $113.15, guaranteed renewable, paid up fully in 20 years

- (Premiums are guaranteed for 5 years not to increase, but may go up every 5 years thereafter) Not all insurance companies offer a limited pay option where the policy is paid up in 20 years.

- Premium payments stop if and when Samantha goes on claim

- Income benefit once she qualifies is $1,500/month or $18,000/year (tax free)

- Monthly benefit is indexed to the Consumer price index up to a maximum of 4% (indexing takes effect once the insured goes on claim)

Payment Options:

Just like other insurance premiums, Samantha could pay for her long-term care policy on a monthly or annual basis out of cash flow. She could also set aside a portion of her assets now to pay the premiums in the future. One very effective way to do this is to purchase a 20-year term-certain annuity that will produce the annual amount of premium she needs to pay. Remember with the policy she selected, she has to make premium payments for only 20 years.

For Samantha this would require the use of $21,939 of her current assets, which represents less that 5% of her net worth. The 20-year term-certain annuity would pay out $1,400 annually for 20 years. If premiums increase above the $1,400 in the future, Samantha will have to come up with the difference out of her cash flow.

Bottom Line:
For a cost of $1,358 per year, Samantha will receive an annual payment of $18,000 (if she goes on claim) to ensure she won't be forced to sell her home. If she requires care for an extended period, the income payments will increase with inflation. After being on claim for 1½ years she will have received all the money back that she paid out in premiums over the 20 years.

Retirement Income Insurance – Explained

What exactly is retirement income insurance and how does it fit into a retirement income plan? I'm willing to bet you've never heard of it. It is a bit obscure. You can't buy it as a standalone insurance policy. Instead, this insurance comes as a feature of a relatively new breed of investment and retirement products. These products are offered by insurance companies and go by such names as Variable Annuities with Living Benefit Riders or

Guaranteed Minimum Withdrawal Benefit Plans (GMWB) or Guaranteed Life Withdrawal Benefit (GLWB).

The most descriptive term is: Guaranteed Living Income Benefit, or GLIB for short. In its basic form a GLIB provides a guaranteed income (usually a percentage of the initial investment – like 5%), paid for life or for a specific period – like 20 years. If this sounds a lot like an annuity, you're right. However, unlike an annuity, which requires you to give your money to the insurance company, a GLIB allows you to retain control of your investment capital, make investment selections within the GLIB and even cash it out if you wish.

The insurance aspect of this product comes from the guaranteed nature of the income received and the costs associated with that guarantee. In addition to standard management fees paid on the investments in a GLIB, you pay an extra fee for the income guarantee. Think of this extra fee as an insurance premium.

These are complex investment products, with many bells and whistles. We won't get into them here. To understand how these products work, let's look at an example of the most basic version of a GLIB.

Retirement Income Insurance (GLIB) – In action

Setting the stage:
Betty and Barney are a married couple, and they are about to retire as they turn 65. They will both collect government pensions. In addition Barney has a modest pension from work. Betty has $125,000 in savings she received from

an inheritance. Barney also has $60,000 in a retirement account (RRSP). They have no debt and own their own home. They live a modest lifestyle and expect to cover their expenses with their pensions and the extra income from Barney's RRSP.

While working, they never had the chance to travel, something they always wanted to do. When they retire they want to make up for it. They don't expect to take elaborate vacations but want to see some of the country. They have set a budget of $3,500 annually for travel expenses. They really want to make this happen and are wondering if a GLIB would allow them to finance their yearly trips.

Solution:
Because they know how much they want to spend annually ($3,500), a GLIB is a good solution. They can invest a specific amount to generate that exact income. They have $125,000 in a taxable investment account, and we know that a basic GLIB will pay out 5% based on the amount invested. If they use $70,000 of that money, they'll be able to produce the $3,500 ($70,000 X 5%) they need. However, this doesn't account for income taxes.

Betty is in a very low tax bracket, because her only other income is a government pension. If we estimate an average tax rate of 20% for Betty, they will need an income of $4,400 to net the $3,500 after tax. Based on this, if Betty invests $88,000 in a GLIB she can generate a guaranteed income of $4,400 for life ($88,000 X 5%= $4,400).

Remember that there is an insurance cost to guarantee this income. In Canada this cost can range from 40 basis points (.40%) to about 95 basis points (.95%). Assuming they use a balanced portfolio as the investment within the GLIB, they will likely pay around 75 basis points (0.75%). With an $88,000 investment this retirement income insurance will cost them $660 ($88,000 X .75%) in the first year.

The dollar amount of this fee is charged annually and changes from year to year, because it's based on the market value of the investment. Some GLIB plans calculate this fee based on the investment value at calendar year end, while others base it upon the anniversary date of the GLIB plan's setup. If the account goes down in value, so will the fee. If it goes up in value, the fee will go up, as well.

Bottom Line:
By using a GLIB, Betty and Barney can ensure that they'll have $3,500 every year for their travel budget. Even if the market crashes, they know they can still go on their annual trip without worry. For them, this peace of mind is well worth the $660 insurance premium for this type of investment.

Appendix #2:

In this appendix I provide a mini case study that compares the requirements to obtain a CFP® designation with another one as found in the FINRA database. Following that, I give you details about the new CFP® requirements that came into effect in Canada in the summer of 2010.

A case study: CFP® vs PRPS

Going through the FINRA database, I found myself comparing other designations, especially those with impressive sounding names, to the CFP® and its stringent requirements. I thought that you might find it helpful if I provided a side-by-side comparison. As an example, Table 10 compares the CFP® with the Personal Retirement Planning Specialist (PRPS) designation. You should check the designations on your prospective advisor's card, as well, to see how they measure up.

Table 10: How the CFP measures up

	CFP®	PRPS
Pre-Requisite/ Experience	-Bachelors degree or higher from an accredited college or university AND - 3 years full-time personal financial planning experience	- Investment advisor license
Educational Requirement	- Complete the CFP board registered program Can qualify to take exam directly if you already have one of the following: -CPA, ChFC, CLU, CFA, PHd in business or economics, Doctor of Business administration, Attorney's License	- 24 hours of live webcasts
Exam Type	- CFP Certification Exam - proctored	- Online, open book exam
Continuing Ed Requirement	- 30 Hours every two years – audited	- 8 hours per year
Accredited by	- National Commission for Certifying Agencies (NCCA)	- none

What does this comparison tell us? First, the PRPS designation can be obtained with relative ease by anyone who has an investment advisors license. No financial planning or industry experience is required. Conceivably, you could obtain your investments license, which has very little to do with retirement planning, today and, within a few days complete the PRPS course, take the open-book exam, and call yourself a Personal Retirement Planning Specialist. Once you have the designation, you have little obligation to keep up with relevant developments as the industry changes, beyond the 8 hours of continuing education each year.

By comparison, the CFP® designation is significantly harder to obtain. As a pre-requisite you must have a bachelor's degree and 3 years of full-time financial planning experience. The course itself is demanding and covers more than 100 topics. When I took the CFP® course in the late 1990s, it took two to three years to complete. First I had to complete all modules, write and pass the module exams, and then write and pass a final proficiency exam. The final exam was six hours long and covered every topic from all the modules.

Since then the course has changed significantly and has become even more difficult. According to the U.S. Certified Financial Planner Board of Standards website, the course will take 18-24 months to complete at an accredited institution. After passing all the courses the CFP® candidate can then apply to write the proficiency exam. Only after passing that exam can she obtain the CFP® certification. Keep in mind that even if she starts the course at the same time as she gets a job in financial planning, she can't get certified until she has acquired at least three years of full-time financial planning experience.

> **By comparison, the CFP® designation is significantly harder to obtain.**

The CFP® requirements in Canada

In Canada, the Financial Planners Standards Council recently updated its requirements for a CFP® designation. As of July 1, 2010, a candidate must complete eight steps to obtain CFP® certification. Here are the steps:

1. Complete an FPSC-approved Core Curriculum education program (or hold a professional designation under the Approved Prior Credential policy)

2. Apply to write the Professional Competence Examination 1 (PCE1). Upon registration for the PCE1, the candidate must register and remain in good standing with the FPSC

3. Pass the PCE1 exam

4. Complete an FPSC-approved Capstone Course and at least one year of financial planning-related work experience

5. Apply to write the Professional Competence Examination 2 (PCE2)

6. Pass the PCE2

7. Complete the remaining two years of financial planning-related work experience

8. Apply to FPSC for CFP® Certification.

Once someone has been granted the right to call himself a CFP® professional he must adhere to a strict code of ethics. This code consists of two parts: Part 1 – principles and part 2 – rules. The 7 principles express the ethical and professional ideals of CFP® professionals in general. The associated rules provide practical guidelines "derived from the tenets embodied in the principles".

The seven principles of the CFP® code of ethics are:

1. **Integrity**: A CFP professional shall always act with integrity.

2. **Objectivity**: A CFP professional shall be objective in providing financial planning to clients.

3. **Competence**: A CFP professional shall provide services to clients competently and maintain the necessary knowledge and skill to continue to do so in those areas in which the CFP professional is engaged.

4. **Fairness**: A CFP professional shall perform financial planning in a manner that is fair and reasonable to clients, principals, partners, and employers and shall disclose conflicts of interest in providing such services.

5. **Confidentiality**: A CFP professional shall maintain confidentiality of all client information.

6. **Professionalism**: A CFP professional's conduct in all matters shall reflect credit upon the profession.

7. **Diligence**: A CFP professional shall act diligently in providing financial planning.

Candidates in the U.S. who pass the final board exam must complete 30 hours of continuing education every two years. In Canada they must complete 30 hours every year, and the Financial Planners Standards Council audits these hours randomly to ensure compliance.

Appendix 3: Worksheets

Included in this appendix are the four worksheets required to create your own Retirement Income Plan as described in chapter 13. They are:

1. Income and Expenses Worksheet

2. Available Assets Worksheet

3. Retirement Spending Funnel

4. Funding Matrix

If you would prefer full size copies of these worksheets they can be downloaded for free at: www.fearlessretirementresources.com

INCOME AND EXPENSE WORKSHEET

INCOME

GUARANTEED INCOME SOURCES	YOU (A)	SPOUSE (B)	COMBINED TOTAL (A+B)*
Government Benefits			
- CPP			
- OAS			
- Social Security			
Employment Pension			
- Workplace 1			
- Workplace 2			
Private Annuities			
- Company 1			
- Company 2			
Foreign Pension			
Other			
Total Guaranteed Income			

EXPENSES

BASIC EXPENSES	YOU (A)	SPOUSE (B)	COMBINED TOTAL (A+B)
Housing			
- Mortgage/Rent Payments			
- Utilities (heat, hydro, water, gas etc.)			
- Phone/Cell/Internet/Cable			
- Property Taxes			
- Condo Fees			
- Maintenance			
- Household Supplies			
Transportation			
- Gas/Fuel			
- Lease Payments			
- Maintenance & Repairs			
- Parking			
- Public Transit			
- Recreational Vehicles			
Daily Living			
- Groceries			
- Clothing			
- Personal Care Items			
Health Care			
- Eye-care/Glasses/Contacts			
- Dental			
- Prescriptions			
Other Expenses You Must Pay			
- Other			
- Other			
- Other			
Total Basic Expenses			

INCOME AND EXPENSE WORKSHEET page 2

WHAT-IF EXPENSES	YOU (A)	SPOUSE (B)	COMBINED TOTAL (A+B)
Home Insurance			
Recreational Property Insurance			
Auto Insurance			
Recreational Vehicle Insurance			
Life Insurance			
Disability Insurance			
Critical Illness Insurance			
Long Term Care Insurance			
Pet Insurance			
Other			
		Total What-If Expenses	

SOCIAL EXPENSES	YOU (A)	SPOUSE (B)	COMBINED TOTAL (A+B)
Recreation and Leisure			
Fitness			
Travel			
Hobbies			
Pets - Food and Vet Bills			
Pets - Boarding			
Education			
Gifts			
Entertainment			
Retaurants/Meals Out			
Annual Club Dues/Memberships			
Subscriptions			
Donations			
Furniture			
Interest on Loans and Credit			
Other		Total Social Expenses	

ESTEEM EXPENSES	YOU (A)	SPOUSE (B)	COMBINED TOTAL (A+B)
Major Purchase			
Elite Club Membership			
Expensive Once in a Lifetime Vacation			
Recreational Property			
Expensive Recreational Vehicle			
Other			
		Total Esteem Expenses	

LEGACY EXPENSES	YOU (A)	SPOUSE (B)	COMBINED TOTAL (A+B)
Charitable Bequest (at death)			
Charitable Gift (while living)			
Life Insurance Proceeds			
Gift of Investments			
Gift of Real Estate			
Other			
		Total Legacy Expenses	

AVAILABLE ASSETS WORKSHEET

RETIREMENT ACCOUNTS - TAX DEFERRED
(Investment Type: Cash, Money Market, GIC, CD, Mutual Fund, Segregated Fund, Stock, Bond etc)

PLAN TYPE	INVESTMENT TYPE	YOUR AMOUNT (A)	YOUR SPOUSE AMOUNT (B)	COMBINED AMOUNT (A+B)*
RRSP				
RRIF				
LIRA				
LIF				
TFSA				
401(K)				
IRA				

*Note: When transferring numbers to the Funding Matrix, use combined amount for both spouses

TAXABLE INVESTMENT ACCOUNTS

INVESTMENT TYPE	OWNERSHIP (YOU OR SPOUSE)	PURCHASE PRICE	CURRENT VALUE*
Cash			
Money Market (like cash)			
GIC (guaranteed investment certificate)			
CD (certificate of deposit)			
Mutual Funds/Segregated Funds			
Stocks			
Bonds			
Other			
Other			
Other			

*Note: Use current values for each type when transferring numbers to the Funding Matrix

REAL ESTATE AND LIFE INSURANCE

LIFE INSURANCE			
TYPE	INSURED PERSON	CASH VALUE	DEATH BENEFIT*
Whole Life			
Universal Life			
Term to 100			
Other			
REAL ESTATE			
TYPE	OWNER	PURCHASE PRICE	CURRENT VALUE*
Home			
Recreational Property			
Rental/Comercial Property			
Other			
Other			

Fearless Retirement Blueprint   Worksheet Series   Financial Doctor Press © 2012

Appendix 3

RETIREMENT SPENDING FUNNEL

Funding Categories   **Expense Categories**   **Gap Analysis**

Guaranteed Income
Government, Work pensions, Annuities →

Basic Expenses
(Food, Gas, Clothing, Shelter, Transportation, Taxes)

Cash, Insurance Premiums →
(House, Auto Life, Disability, Critical Illness, Long-term Care)

"What If" Expenses
(Damage, Illness, Injury, etc.)

Non-Guaranteed Income
From Investments →

Social Expenses
(Entertainment, Vacations, Sports)

Income Gap Calculator
Guaranteed Income − Expenses

Gap (±) =

Sale of Investments →

Esteem Expenses
(Luxury Car, Rv, Boat, Exclusive Club Membership)

+ You have an excess income
− You have a gap that needs to be filled

Final Estate
Sale of Investments, Real Estate, Life Insurance Proceeds →

Legacy

Lump Sum Needs Calculator
Esteem + Legacy

= Lump Sum Need

Fearless Retirement Blueprint   Worksheet Series   Financial Doctor Press © 2012

FUNDING MATRIX

	RETIREMENT ACCOUNTS					TAXABLE INVESTMENT ACCOUNTS					LIFE INSURANCE		REAL ESTATE			INCOME GAP
																ESTEEM EXPENSES
						YOUR AVAILABLE ASSETS										LEGACY EXPENSES
	RRSP	RRIF	LIRA	TFSA	401K	IRA	CASH	BONDS	GIC'S	CD'S	STOCKS	MUTUAL FUNDS	WHOLE LIFE	UNIVERSAL LIFE	COMMERCIAL	RECREATIONAL	HOME

PRODUCT OPTIONS (FROM YOUR PRODUCT ALLOCATION)

														LEGACY FUNDING		
LEGACY														LIFE INS INVESTMENTS	REAL ESTATE	
ESTEEM														TOTAL ESTEEM EXPENSE FUNDING		
SWP																
ANNUITY																
GLIB																
TOTAL																

INCOME OPTIONS (FROM YOUR CALCULATIONS)

							TOTAL INCOMES	
							GUARANTEED	VARIABLE
SWP								
ANNUITY								
GLIB								
OTHER								
SUB TOTALS								

GROSS INCOME FROM ALLOCATION	
TAXES	
NET AVAILABLE TO SPEND	

Fearless Retirement Blueprint Worksheet Series Financial Doctor Press © 2012

Statement of DISCLAIMER

This book and its associated websites www.fearlessretirement.com and www.fearlessretirementresources.com are intended to provide authoritative and reliable information regarding retirement income planning in today's financial environment. Situations and recommendations may change based on legislative amendments or the availability of new financial service products in the marketplace.

The book and related material on the websites was created with the understanding that neither the Author nor the Publisher is engaged in rendering legal, accounting, financial, investment or any other professional advice or services by publishing these materials. A professional in any of the above stated areas of specialization should be consulted regarding questions pertaining to any individuals personal finances. Each individual's financial situation should be carefully considered to reflect those particular criteria before considering any financial strategy.

Readers should be aware that investment markets have inherent risks and there can be no guarantee of future profits. Likewise, past performance does not ensure future results.

Recommendations are subject to change at any time. Mutual funds are sold by prospectus, and Segregated Funds (variable annuities) by information folder.

Case studies and examples in this book are hypothetical in nature and are not based on real people or clients of the author. They were used for illustrative purposes only as a way to further explain concepts presented in this work

The Author and Publisher specifically disclaim any liability, loss, or risk that is incurred as a consequence, directly or indirectly, of the use and application of any of the contents of this work.

Although the author, Conrad Toner is a Mutual Fund Representative with Investia Financial Services Inc., Investia Financial Services Inc. has not approved nor does it endorse the content or any recommendations and/or opinions contained in this publication.